T0006725

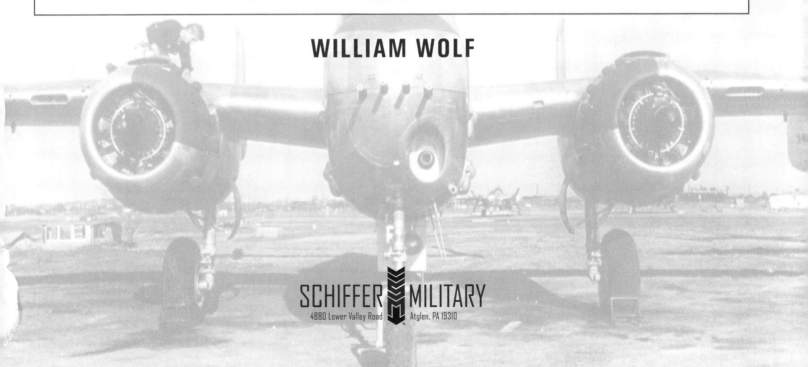

LEGENDS OF WARFARE

AVIATION

B-25 Mitchell, Vol. 2

The G through J, F-10, and PBJ Models in World War II

WILLIAM WOLF

SCHIFFER MILITARY

4880 Lower Valley Road   Atglen, PA 19310

Designed by Justin Watkinson
Front cover image courtesy of Rich Kolasa
Type set in Impact/Minion Pro/Univers LT Std

ISBN: 978-0-7643-6342-9
Printed in India

Published by Schiffer Publishing, Ltd.
4880 Lower Valley Road
Atglen, PA 19310
Phone: (610) 593-1777; Fax: (610) 593-2002
Email: Info@schifferbooks.com
www.schifferbooks.com

For our complete selection of fine books on this and related subjects, please visit our website at www.schifferbooks.com. You may also write for a free catalog.

Schiffer Publishing's titles are available at special discounts for bulk purchases for sales promotions or premiums. Special editions, including personalized covers, corporate imprints, and excerpts, can be created in large quantities for special needs. For more information, contact the publisher.

We are always looking for people to write books on new and related subjects. If you have an idea for a book, please contact us at proposals@schifferbooks.com.

Acknowledgments

Most color photographs of aircraft in this book are of the Commemorative Air Force (CAF) Arizona Wing's "Maid in the Shade," Jack Fedor's "Barbie III," and the Mid-Atlantic Air Museum's (MAAM) "Briefing Time," and their excellent website. I would like to thank Russell Strine, then president of the MAAM; Jack Fedor and Bill Harris of Warbirds Unlimited; and Kimberley Ring of the AZ CAF for their help and permission to use photos and materials about their museums' aircraft. In the early 1970s, I was fortunate to have access to the photo scrapbooks of Mike Rice, who was a former B-25 mechanic and absolute North American Airlines (NAA) aircraft aficionado, of the B-25 in particular. Mr. Rice documented the gamut of NAA aircraft through NAA, USAAF, and newspaper and magazine photos and articles. Thanks also go to the personnel at the Albert F. Simpson Historical Research Center (ASHRC), Maxwell AFB, Alabama; the Museum of the US Air Force Archives at Wright-Patterson, Dayton, Ohio; the National Archives; the Library of Congress (LoC) as the source for color and black-and-white photos of North American facilities; the Ferndale photographic facility, located in Washington, DC; and the Pima Air and Space Museum, Tucson, Arizona, where I copied thousands of photos and reams of data. For the twenty-second time, thanks go to my persevering wife, Nancy, who allows me to spend many hours researching and writing and patiently (mostly) waits while I browse bookstores and visit air museums and government facilities in search of new material and photos.

Contents

Introduction

On April 18, 1942, sixteen modified North American B-25B Mitchell medium bombers, led by Lt. Col. James (Jimmy) Doolittle, are seen poised for takeoff from the carrier USS *Hornet* to bomb five Japanese cities, including Tokyo. Although the damage inflicted was materially light, news of the raid boosted the flagging morale of Americans, who had heard nothing but the bad news of Japanese successes during the four and a half months after the Pearl Harbor disaster. *AAF*

Of all the medium bombers of World War II, Axis and Allied, the B-25 probably was the most formidable and adaptable of any. Like its blue-collar big brother, the B-24 Liberator, so well known for its attack on the Ploesti Oil Refineries during August 1943, the B-25 established its reputation during one iconic attack: the celebrated Doolittle "Thirty Seconds over Tokyo" mission of April 18, 1942. The 9,880 Mitchells built were flown by the US Army, Navy, and Marine Air Forces, and additionally by the British, Australians, Polish, French, Dutch, Soviets, Brazilians, and Chinese. This versatile bomber served the European theater of operations (ETO), the Mediterranean theater of operations (MTO), North Africa, and, most importantly, in the Pacific. Wherever it served it had a profound influence, assuming many roles, beginning its combat career as a standard medium bomber and then finding its niche as a feared, heavily armed, low-altitude strafer and bomber. Enemy shipping in the Mediterranean and Pacific suffered its wrath in skip-bombing attacks, while bridges in Italy and Burma collapsed under its attacks. Throughout the Pacific and Chinese-Burma-India theater of operations (CBI), its parafrag bombs, multiple machine guns, and even a large nose-mounted 75 mm cannon were the scourge of Japanese sailors and soldiers.

Just as the B-24 archetype was pictured over the burning Romanian Ploesti Oil Fields during the Tidal Wave raid of August 1, 1943, the representative combat undertaking of the B-25 was pictured in the numerous photos taken from bomber's tail strike cameras of parafrag bombs floating down on parachutes toward Japanese aircraft and shipping and infantry positions. Flying in the Pacific with Gen. Kenney's 5th Air Force, the Mitchell was arguably the major bomber airpower factor in the Southwest Pacific campaign. *AAF*

B-25s Featured in This Book

CAF Arizona Wing B-25J, "Maid in the Shade"

The B-25J "Maid in the Shade" (43-35972) is an airworthy B-25J owned and operated by the Arizona Wing of the Commemorative Air Force (AZ CAF). It is restored to its 1944 combat configuration of the 437th Bomb Squadron, 319th Bomb Group, 12th Air Force, which was based on Corsica during 1944–45, where it flew fifteen combat missions, mainly against railway bridges. The aircraft is available for rides for seven passengers at the CAF Arizona Wing Museum, located at Falcon Field, Mesa, Arizona. *Author / AZ CAF*

Warbirds Unlimited's B-25H, "Barbie III"

The second H model off the NAA assembly line, "Barbie III" (43-4106), is the only 75 mm cannon–equipped B-25H in existence. This particular B-25H served stateside until 1947, when it was declared surplus and sold it to the Bendix Corporation, which used it for ten years as a test aircraft. It then went through a dozen owners and was finally restored to its "Barbie III" H configuration by Warbirds Unlimited's Jack Fedor. At the time of my B-25 research, it was based at Falcon Field, Mesa, Arizona, and owned and operated by Fedor, who generously gave me total access to the aircraft. It is currently owned by the Cavanaugh Flight Museum, Addison, Texas, and is not now airworthy. *Author / Fedor Barbie III*

Mid-Atlantic Air Museum (MAAM) B-25J, "Briefing Time"

B-25J-25-NC (44-29939) was used as a postwar pilot trainer until 1958, when it was placed in storage. After being declared surplus in 1959, it was owned by Tallmantz Studios, famous for supplying aircraft and stunt pilots to the movie industry. It served as support aircraft for *Catch-22*, *Around the World in 80 Days*, and other films. After having several more owners, it was donated to the Mid-Atlantic Air Museum (MAAM) in 1981, where it was restored as "Briefing Time" (44-29939), which served with the 489 Bomb Squadron, 340th Bomb Group, 57th Bomb Wing, 12th Air Force, where it flew combat in the North African and Italian campaigns. "Briefing Time" is currently in airworthy status at the MAAM, located at Reading Regional Airport–Spaatz Field in Berks County, Pennsylvania. The MAAM has a superb online "Briefing Time" virtual tour and is available for aircraft tours but not rides. *MAAM*

CHAPTER 1

The Weapon Is Armed and Strikes

B-25G: The First of the Fearsome Mitchells

The B-25G (NA-96) was the first Mitchell to mount a standard Army 75 mm M4 cannon that was intended for antishipping attacks in the Pacific. The B-25G retained the B-25C Bendix dorsal and ventral turrets aft of the nose, but the ventral turret was often deleted in the field and was officially deleted on the B-25G production line, effective with aircraft 42-65001. The supplementary forward-firing machine gun armament of the B-25G was considered to be inadequate, and two more nose guns were added and four more guns in blister packs were mounted on the fuselage sides. Many B-25Gs were also provided with a twin .50-caliber tail turret in the field to counterbalance the additional weight of the six extra .50s mounted in the nose and blister packs. A single .50 was mounted at the right and left waist stations. When enemy targets suitable for cannon attack disappeared, the cannon was removed from eighty-two B-25Gs, with a pair of additional .50s installed in the nose tunnel where the cannon had been located. The standard bomb bay was retained but was modified for the installation of a standard aircraft torpedo.

The modified B-25G made its initial flight on October 2, 1942, and testing revealed that because of the additional weight and drag, maximum speed fell to 278 mph, but the stall characteristics were normal and diving at speeds of up to 340 mph was tolerated.

The B-25G five-man crew consisted of the pilot, copilot, navigator/cannoneer, dorsal turret gunner, and radio operator. Since there was no bombardier, the pilot fired the nose armament and released the bombs, while the radio operator also served as the ventral turret gunner.

After successful test flights, the Army Air Corps (ACC) ordered 400 without lower turrets, with the first five and an additional fifty-eight being B-25C-NAs modified mostly in Kansas City and redesignated as B-25Gs.

B-25G Specifications

North American Model	Number NA-96
US Navy/Marine designation	PBJ-1G* (1 ordered by BuAER)
Contract no. (date)	AC-27390 (3/28/42)
Number built	400**
First flight (pilot)	October 22, 1942 (Edward Virgin)
First delivery / last delivery	May 1943 / August 1943
Crew (5)	pilot, copilot, navigator/cannoneer, dorsal turret gunner, radio operator (ventral turret gunner)**
Engines	Wright R-2600-13
Max. hp	1,700 (each)
Carburetor	Holley 1685HA
Maximum speed	281 mph @ 15,000 feet
Initial rate of climb	967 feet per minute
Ceiling	24,300 feet
Combat range	1,535 miles***
Fuel load	670 gallons in 4 inner wing panel tanks
	515 gallons in bomb bay (ferrying)****
Dimensions	Length: 50 feet, 10 inches
	Height: 16 feet, 4.2 inches
	Wingspan: 67 feet, 6.7 inches
	Wing area: 610 square feet
Empty weight	19,975 pounds
Maximum takeoff weight	35,000 pounds
Armament B-25C conversions	1 75 mm cannon in nose
	2 .50-caliber fixed machine guns in nose
	Dorsal: 2 .50-caliber machine gun Bendix turret
	Ventral: 2 .50-caliber mgs in retractable Bendix turret
Armament B-25G-5 (42-65001 onward)	same as C conversions, with ventral turret deleted

* Only one PBJ-1 G, BuAer no. 35097 (former USAAF serial number 42-65031), was acquired by the USN Bureau of Aeronautics.
** The ventral turret was deleted from production after the last B-25G-5 (#42-65001) and onward.
*** With 974 gallons of fuel and a 3,200-pound bombload. Range figures varied considerably depending on the amount of fuel carried and payload.
    Additionally, there was one XB-25G prototype and five service test aircraft. Sixty-three existing B-25Cs were also modified to B-25G standards.
**** Later versions had the following: 125 gallons in side waist positions (ferry)
        215 gallons in bomb bay (self-sealing)
        335-gallon droppable metal tank in waist (ferry)
        Varying auxiliary tanks in outer wing panels

The XB-25G was first flown during October 1942 and NAA's B-25C contract was modified to convert 400 to the B-25G configuration from May to August 1943, with a further sixty-three C's converted to G standards. *AAF*

The armament of the B-25G-5 (42-65001 onward) was the same as C conversions (*left*), with ventral turret deleted (*right photo*). *NAA/Rice*

The B-25Gs that were B-25C conversions featured a 75 mm cannon in the nose, two .50-caliber fixed machine guns in the nose, a dorsal Bendix turret with two .50-caliber machine guns, and a ventral retractable Bendix turret with two .50-caliber machine guns (seen as ventral midfuselage bulge on photo). *NAA/Rice*

The B-25G (NA-96) was the first Mitchell to mount a standard Army 75 mm M4 cannon (the heaviest US aerial gun of the war), which was intended for antishipping attacks in the Pacific. For testing, B-25C-1-NA (41-13296) was modified to the lone XB-25G standard. The former bombardier glazed nose was replaced with an armored solid nose shortened by the aerodynamic maximum of 26 inches, which reduced the bomber's overall length to 51 feet. *NAA/Rice*

B-25H: Fourteen Formidable .50-Caliber Machine Guns and a 75 mm Cannon

Although the cannon-carrying B-25G had not met expectations, nonetheless 1,000 improved cannon-carrying attack strafers were ordered under the designation B-25H, with the M4 cannon replaced by a lighter Oldsmobile T13E1 75 mm cannon. The B-25H nose was armed with four rather than two .50-caliber guns, each carrying 400 rounds. The first 300 B-25Hs had two .50-caliber side blister guns on the right side only, with the remaining 700 aircraft having the blister guns installed on both sides. Two .50 machine guns were provided at the waist stations, installed on flexible mounts behind slightly staggered, large, cylindrically shaped "bay windows," firing through sockets cut into their lower rear corners. The dorsal turret was moved forward on the fuselage to a position above the navigator's station, and the fuselage was slightly lowered to make room for twin .50-caliber tail guns and to maintain the correct balance against the additional weight added to the rear by the new waist guns and tail turret. The retractable Bendix ventral turret was finally eliminated. The B-25H carried the amazingly powerful armament of fourteen .50-inch machine guns and a 75 mm cannon and could also carry up to 3,200 pounds of bombs or a 2,000-pound torpedo. (Individual B-25H armament is depicted and discussed elsewhere.)

Production B-25Hs were flown by a five-man crew: pilot, navigator / radio operator / cannoneer, flight engineer / dorsal gunner, midships gunner / camera operator, and tail gunner. One of the more controversial changes introduced by the B-25H was the deletion of the copilot and his seat, armor plate, and controls, resulting in a reduction of over 450 pounds. A jump seat was provided for the navigator at the copilot position, since his place had been appropriated by the dorsal turret's movement forward.

The first production B-25H (43-4105) was flown for the first time on July 31, 1943, and the first B-25H was accepted by the AAF in August 1943. The last B-25H-10-NA manufactured at the Inglewood plant was also the last B-25 produced there before NAA converted to the manufacture of the P-51 Mustang. The last B-25H was accepted in July 1944, but by that time, combat reports established that the cannon-armed B-25H offered no particular advantage over specially adapted strafers armed exclusively with machine guns. By that time, targets appropriate for cannon attack were relatively scarce, and many targets that were vulnerable to the cannon were also vulnerable to a battery of .50-caliber machine guns or to bombs. Consequently, the use of the heavy cannon was generally abandoned in the Southwest Pacific by August 1944 but continued on with the 14th Air Force in China and the 1st Air Commando Group in Burma.

Author / Fedor Barbie III

B-25H Specifications

North American Model Number	NA-98
US Navy/Marine designation	PBJ-1H (236 ordered by BuAER)
British designation	None
Contract no. (date)	AC-30478 (6/20/42)
Number built	1,000
First flight (pilot)	XB-25H, May 15, 1943 (Edward Virgin)
	B-25H, July 31, 1943 (Robert Chilton)
First delivery / last delivery	August 1943 / July 1944
Crew (5)	pilot, navigator, radio operator / cannoneer, flight engineer / dorsal gunner, amidships gunner / camera operator, tail gunner
Engines	Wright R-2600-13
Max. hp	1,700 (each)
Carburetor	Holley 1685HA
Maximum speed	275 mph @ 13,000 feet
Initial rate of climb	790 feet per minute
Ceiling	24,800 feet
Combat range	1,350 miles*
Fuel load	670 gallons in 4 inner wing panel tanks
	304 gallons in auxiliary outer panel wing tanks
	125 gallons in side waist positions (ferry)
	215 gallons in bomb bay (self-sealing)
	515 gallons in bomb bay (ferry)
	335 gallons in metal droppable bomb bay
Dimensions	same as B-25G
Empty weight	19,975 pounds
Maximum takeoff weight	33,500 pounds
Armament B-25H	1 75 mm cannon in the nose
	4 fixed .50-caliber machine guns in the nose
	2 fixed .50-caliber machine guns in the right blisters
	2 .50-caliber machine guns dorsal Bendix turret
	2 .50-caliber machine guns waist positions
	2 .50-caliber machine guns in tail turret
Armament B-25H-5 (43-4405) onward:	same as B-25H plus two fixed .50-caliber machine guns in left blisters

* With 974 gallons of fuel and a 3,000-pound bombload. Range figures varied considerably depending on the amount of fuel carried and payload.

The first production B-25H (43-4105) was first flown on July 31, 1943, and the first B-25H of 1,000 was accepted by the AAF, in August 1943. The last B-25H-10-NA manufactured at the Inglewood plant was also the last B-25 produced there before NAA converted to the manufacture of the P-51 Mustang. The US Navy/Marine designation was PBJ-1H of which 236 were ordered by the BuAER. *AAF*

The forward-firing armament of the B-25H was a 75 mm cannon in the nose, four fixed .50-caliber machine guns in the nose, and two fixed .50-caliber machine guns in the right blisters (and later two in the left) as well on the side of the fuselage. *Author / Fedor Barbie III*

The dorsal turret was moved forward on the fuselage to a position above the navigator's station. *Author / Fedor Barbie III*

B-25J: The Final and Most Numerous and Heavily Armed Mitchell

The B-25J (NA-108) was the final and most heavily armed Mitchell production model and also was the version built in the largest numbers, with 4,318 built (the USMC ordered 255 B-25Js under the designation PBJ-1J). It was manufactured solely by NAA Kansas City, which briefly simultaneously built both the B-25D and J, with the first J being accepted in December 1943 and the last D completed in March 1944. The first B-25J (43-3780) first flew in October 1943, the first AAF acceptance took place before the end of that year, and the last B-25J was delivered to the AAF in August 1945. There were two basic versions of the B-25J, with the only actual difference between the two being the type of nose installation: the "greenhouse" bomber version or the solid-nose eight-gun "strafer" version.

The major B-25J modification concerned its restoration to the original medium-bomber role, reverting to the transparent, bombardier-equipped nose of the earlier B-25C and D. During midproduction the single flexible-nose .50 was augmented by a second .50 fixed machine gun installed in the glazed nose, with the flexible nose gun relocated 4 inches higher. The normal bombload was 3,000 pounds, but a maximum bombload of 4,000 pounds could be carried on shorter-range missions in combinations of larger and smaller bombs of various types, including parafrags. A normal offensive load of two 1,600- or three 1,000-pound bombs could be carried internally.

Author/CAF

AAF

B-25J Specifications

North American Model Number	NA-108
US Navy/Marine designation	PBJ-1J (244 ordered by BuAER)
British designations	Mitchell III (314 ordered)
Contract no. (date)	AC-19341 (4/14/43)
Number delivered	4,318*
First flight (pilot)	March 3, 1943 (Joseph Barton)
First delivery / last delivery	December 1943 / August 1945
Crew (6)	pilot, copilot, navigator/bombardier/gunner, engineer / dorsal turret gunner, radio gunner / waist gunner, tail gunner
Engine	Wright R-2600-29
Max. hp	1,700 (each)
Maximum speed	293 mph @ 13,850 feet
Initial rate of climb	1,587 feet per minute
Ceiling	24,500 feet
Combat range	1,350 miles**
Fuel load	670 gallons in 4 inner wing panel tanks
	304 gallons in auxiliary outer panel wing tanks
	125 gallons in side waist positions (ferry)
	215 gallons in bomb bay (self-sealing)
	515 gallons in bomb bay (ferry)
	35 gallons in metal droppable bomb bay
Dimensions	Length: 53 feet, 5.75 inches
	Height: 16 feet, 4.2 inches
	Wingspan: 67 feet, 6.7 inches
	Wing area: 610 square feet
Empty weight	19,490 pounds
Maximum takeoff weight	33,400 pounds
Armament	1 flexible .50-caliber machine gun in the nose or replaced by 4 fixed .50-caliber machine guns in a solid factory-prefabricated nose
	2 fixed .50-caliber machine guns each in the right and left blisters
	2 .50-caliber machine guns in dorsal Bendix turret
	2 .50-caliber machine guns in the 2 waist positions
	2 .50-caliber machine guns in tail turret

* 4,390 built, but only 4,318 delivered
** With 974 gallons of fuel and a 3,000-pound bombload. Range figures varied considerably depending on the amount of fuel carried and payload.

The B-25J, the most recognizable of all B-25 models, was really a combination of the best features of the B-25H-NA strafer and the B-25D-NC bomber, being the most heavily armed B-25 to date and returning to its primary function as medium bomber by reverting to the transparent, bombardier-equipped nose of the earlier B-25C and D. It had improved bomb platform stability and was outstanding in speed, performance at altitude, visibility and night flying, and short-field characteristics. *AAF*

In both J versions the copilot position (omitted on the B-25H) was restored, with the crew now six: pilot, copilot, navigator/bombardier/gunner, turret gunner / engineer, radio operator / waist gunner, and tail gunner. In both B-25J versions, the tail gun position with the deeper rear fuselage, the bay-window-mounted waist guns, and the forward-mounted dorsal turret that had been introduced on the B-25H were all retained. *AAF*

The transparent nose, with its bombardier, could be replaced at the factory by a solid nose that was equipped with six or eight .50-caliber machine guns. *AAF*

F-10 Photo-Recon Version

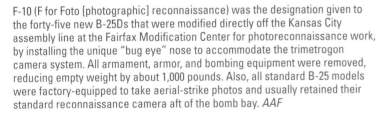

F-10 (F for Foto [photographic] reconnaissance) was the designation given to the forty-five new B-25Ds that were modified directly off the Kansas City assembly line at the Fairfax Modification Center for photoreconnaissance work, by installing the unique "bug eye" nose to accommodate the trimetrogon camera system. All armament, armor, and bombing equipment were removed, reducing empty weight by about 1,000 pounds. Also, all standard B-25 models were factory-equipped to take aerial-strike photos and usually retained their standard reconnaissance camera aft of the bomb bay. *AAF*

The F-10 had crew of five: pilot, copilot, navigator, radio operator, and photographer. The navigator was particularly important, since he needed to determine accurate altitudes and flight paths and to identify known landmarks and waypoints. The Mitchell's stability, which made it an outstanding bombing platform, also made it an excellent aerial photographic aircraft. The F-10s were ordered principally for photo mapping and charting, since large areas of the earth's surface had never been accurately mapped and charted, and also to update obsolete maps and charts. A single B-25D/F-10-NC flying at 200 mph could map 20,000 square miles in four hours. The missions were often long (up to ten hours) and flew over large areas of uncharted mountains or jungle, where a downed aircraft could vanish without a trace. *AAF*

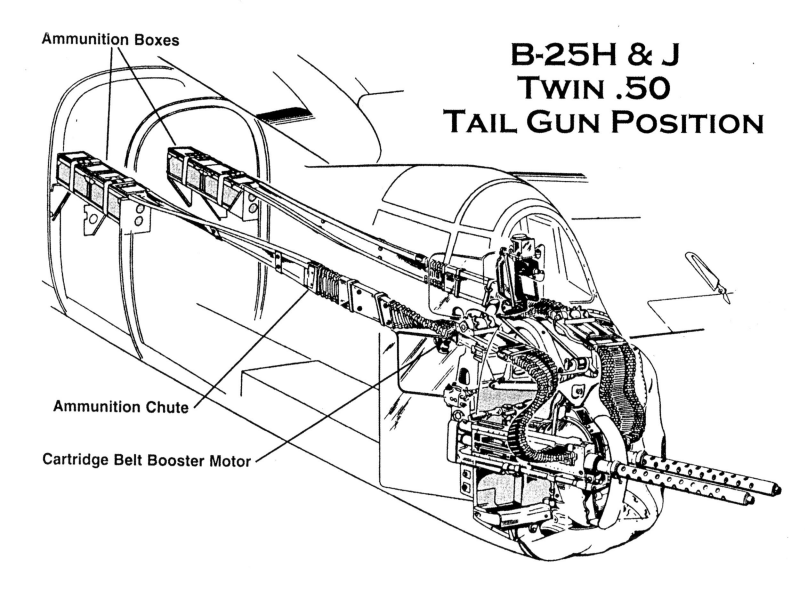

Ammunition Boxes

B-25H & J
Twin .50
Tail Gun Position

Ammunition Chute

Cartridge Belt Booster Motor

Many of the PBJ-1C and D versions carried a bulbous APS-3 search radar antenna protruding from the upper part of the transparent nose. Large 11.75-inch Tiny Tim rockets can be seen attached under the fuselage for antishipping operations. *USMC*

PBJ-1 (USN): In mid-1942, the PBJ had its beginning with the USN due to the AAF interservice agreement, during which the Navy exchanged the Boeing plant in Renton, Washington, for the Kansas City plant for B-29 Superfortress production. The Navy's Boeing XPBB Sea Ranger flying boat, produced at Renton, was competing for B-29 Wright R-3350 engines and was canceled in return for part of the Kansas City Mitchell production. Other terms included the interservice transfer of fifty B-25Cs and 152 B-25Ds to the Navy. The bombers carried Navy Bureau Numbers (BuNos), beginning with BuNo 34998.

On USMC PBJ-1Hs and Js, the APS-3 search radar antenna was usually housed inside a ventral or wingtip radome. *USMC*

VIP Transport Conversions

Between 1942 and 1949, NAA converted six B-25s to RB-25 personal transports. Two were converted for NAA corporate use and three as VIP transports (two as the personal aircraft of Gen. Arnold and one for Gen. Eisenhower); the sixth conversion was an NAA postwar combination conversion to be used as a sales tool to convince potential civilian buyers to purchase a corporate transport, and to convince military buyers to purchase it as a twin-engine training aircraft.

Whiskey Express: "Dutch's Airplane"

The first NAA executive transport was also the first B-25 (40-2165); it was taken directly off the production line and was initially used for general testing by the AAC. On November 9, 1942, after testing, it was returned to NAA and converted to VIP transport status and irreverently and unofficially named the "Whiskey Express" but since it was used mostly by NAA president Dutch Kindelberger, it was usually called "Dutch's Airplane." *NAA/Rice*

All military equipment was removed and a set of four windows were installed in the rear fuselage; five passenger seats were mounted in the rear fuselage, as were a desk and an intercom system. Two more seats were installed forward of the bomb bay, directly behind the flight deck, and a bunk was fitted into the crawlspace above the bomb bay, which was also used as a baggage hold. Other modifications were to the bombardier's greenhouse nose, which was faired over by a solid nose to house the navigation and radio equipment. The "Whiskey Express" flew in its full AAF insignia array, and the tail numbers remained painted on the aircraft. After flying Kindelberger and other company personnel on many trips over the US, on January 8, 1945, it suffered a hydraulic system failure and was damaged beyond repair in a crash landing and had to be scrapped. *NAA/Rice*

In early 1943, Gen. H. H. "Hap" Arnold visited Dutch Kindelberger at the NAA Inglewood plant and was impressed by "Dutch's Airplane." Eisenhower approved the funds and the transfer of the fourth B-25 built (40-2168) back to NAA for an identical conversion for his personal transport. *NAA/Rice*

Hap's RB-25C was one of the original nine 0-degree constant-dihedral B-25s and was retrofitted with the gull wing. In mid-1944, Gen. Arnold traded in this personal transport for a newly converted RB-25J (44-28945) (*shown*), with NAA duplicating almost all the modifications that had been included in Gen. Eisenhower's B-25J. The extent to which Arnold actually used this VIP version in not known, but during January 1946 it was released back to general service and was redesignated VB-25J for personnel transportation. *NAA/Rice*

Hap Arnold's B-25 is now the oldest example of the B-25 still in existence. Built in 1940–41, after the war it was purchased surplus and was owned by Howard Hughes in the 1950s, and then by various civilian owners through the 1980s until purchased by Jeff Clyman, founder of the well-known flight jacket company Avirex Ltd., in 1989. Clyman donated to the American Airpower Museum Farmingdale, New York, and has been flying to air shows as "Miss Hap" throughout the country for over thirty years. *American Air Power Museum*

During February 1944, NAA was contracted to convert a B-25J-1 as the personal transport for Gen. Eisenhower. No. 43-4030 was selected to be modified as North American's third conversion, and the aircraft was improved to duplicate a commercial airliner. Eisenhower is reported to have used this plane on only a few occasions, and during the D-day invasion he was flown over the beaches in a specially modified two seat P-51 Mustang. *NAA/Rice*

ACM Sir Arthur Tedder, the Allied MTO CG, was transported by B-25G-5 (42-65094; no RAF serial), which had all military equipment removed, including its 75 mm cannon; also, the muzzle opening faired over, the tail gun position was modified, and rather basic seating was added to its interior. *Author*

On November 28, 1947, famed World War II French general Philippe Leclerc, inspector of land forces in North Africa, and his staff were transported in his personal B-25D-10 (ex-41-30330) (F-RAFC) GLAM I/40 ELA, "Tailly II." While en route from Oran, Algeria, the aircraft encountered a sandstorm, causing the pilot to reduce altitude in an attempt to establish visual contact with the ground, but the plane crashed in a large explosion that killed all crew and nine passengers in French Algeria. *Author*

Experimental Mitchells

NA-98 "Super Strafer"

NAA "Super Strafer" was to feature ten forward-firing guns, with eight .50-caliber guns in a solid nose (and 75 mm) and two .50-caliber dorsal turret guns, while the fourteen-gun forward-firing version would reemploy the four guns in the two blister packs. In addition, there were two .50-caliber tail guns and two .50 waist guns, for a total of eighteen guns. A bomber version had a glazed nose with two fixed and one guided machine gun (300 rounds per barrel). *NAA/Rice*

After Douglas had introduced its costly, heavily armed A-26 Invader in early 1944, the Air Materiel Command requested that NAA submit a proposal for an improved, less costly attack bomber that would provide the firepower of the B-25H strafers but also deliver significantly improved performance from the 2,000 hp Pratt & Whitney Double Wasp R-2800s that had become available and replaced the Wright R-2600s. B-25H (43-4406), the 302nd H off the production line, was selected to be modified as the NA-98X prototype. Except for the removal of the fuselage blister gun pack, the aircraft had the same armament (including the 75 mm cannon) as the B-25H. *NAA/Rice*

On April 24, 1944, Maj. Perry Ritchie destroyed the NA-98 during an ill-advised low-level buzz over Mines Field that stressed the aircraft's structural limits. *NAA/Rice*

XB-28 (NA-63) Dragon

The XB-28 (NA-63) Dragon was North American's response to an order for a high-altitude medium bomber issued on February 13, 1940, with three prototypes being ordered: 40-3056, 40-3057, and 40-3058 (as the XB-28A reconnaissance version).

The camo-finish XB-28 high-altitude medium bomber, which first flew on April 26, 1942, was based on the B-25 design, but as it evolved it became a completely new single-tail design that resembled the Martin B-26 Marauder and was one of the first combat aircraft with a pressurized cabin. Its pair of turbosupercharged 2,000 hp Pratt & Whitney R-2800 Double Wasp engines supplied it with substantially more power than the B-25's Wright R-2600s. The second medium-bomber prototype was canceled. *NAA/Rice*

The NMF XB-28A reconnaissance version, the third prototype, crashed during testing on August 4, 1943, into the Pacific, off Southern California, after the crew bailed out. Although the XB-28 proved an excellent design and its high-altitude performance greatly surpassed that of the B-25; at the time, most medium bombing was from relatively low altitudes, and the improvements in its high-altitude performance were not considered sufficient to justify the interruption of B-25 production for an untried type, and the project was canceled. *NAA/Rice*

NAA offered a standard-production B-25C-10 (42-32281) as the XB-25E to be modified for anti-icing research, with a heated wing. Extensive modifications were made inside the wing to allow for the movement of air heated by exhaust gases, and the engine cowlings were modified to provide the air to be heated for the system. A heat exchanger was installed to the exhaust, and control valves were placed to control air flow. *NAA/Rice*

Modifications to the aircraft nicknamed "Flamin' Mamie" were completed in early in 1944, and in late February, after NAA flight testing, it was flown to the Ice Research Base near Minneapolis, Minnesota. Through the rest of 1945 and 1946, NACA used the XB-25E extensively for icing research, developing improved anti-icing systems and weather-sensing instruments for flight planning. Testing with the XB-25E would continue until February 1953, when it was returned to the USAF at Wright Field. The bundled-up crew is pictured posing with "Mamie." *NAA/Rice*

"Flamin Mamie" arrived at the Lewis Ice Research Center, Cleveland, during July 1944, and remained there until February 1953, when she was returned to the USAF. She is shown in the late 1940s with revised nose art, larger propeller blades, leading edge heating units, and an electrically heated plastic nose coat. *NACA*

B-25s in Foreign Service

B-25s in English (RAF) Service

Mitchell Mk. I: The Royal Air Force (RAF) was an early Lend-Lease purchaser of the B-25, with the first Mitchell Is delivered during August 1941 to No. 111 Operational Training Unit, based in the Bahamas, where they were used exclusively for training and never reached operational status. The RAF would be the only Allied air force to use the B-25 operationally from UK bases, since the AAF used the Martin B-26 Marauder instead in the medium-bomber role. *AFHRC*

Mitchell Mk. II: The predominant RAF B-25 version was the Mitchell II, which was equivalent to the AAF's B-25C (Inglewood) and B-25D (Kansas City). Altogether, 167 B-25Cs and 371 B-25Ds were delivered to the RAF. *AFHRC*

Mitchell Mk. III: The final RAF B-25 purchase was the Mitchell III, which was the USAAF B-25J, with deliveries taking place between August 1944 and August 1945. The Mitchell IIIs were issued as replacement aircraft for 2nd Group's Mitchell IIs. Some 910 Lend-Lease Mitchells were delivered to the RAF, including fifty-six Mk. Is, 538 Mk. IIs, and 316 Mk. IIIs (as B-25Js). The RAF tested the cannon-armed G series but did not adopt them or the following H series. The typical Lend-Lease cost was $99,000 per aircraft. *AFHRC*

Foreign-Flown B-25s in RAF Service

Polish B-25s RAF Service

During September and October 1943, the RAF Polish 305 Squadron became part of the newly formed 2nd Tactical Air Force, which flew tactical air missions on critical enemy targets (such as bridges, transport, communications, etc.) on the Continent. During this time the squadron converted briefly to Mitchell IIs before adopting the Mosquito FB.VI, which it operated for the remainder of the European campaign. *AFHRC*

Dutch B-25s in RAF Service

During June 1940, former Royal Dutch Naval Air Service personnel who had escaped to England after the German occupation of Holland were formed as RAF No. 320 Squadron, equipped with various British aircraft, flying antisubmarine patrols, convoy escort missions, and air-sea rescue missions. They transitioned to the Mitchell II in September 1943, operating over the Continent against German tactical targets such as transport, rail and road, and communication targets. The squadron moved to Belgium during October 1944 and converted to the Mitchell III in 1945. *AFHRC*

B-25s in Australian (RAAF) Service

The Royal Australian Air Force (RAAF) did not take the B-25 Mitchell into inventory until May 1944, when its No. 2 Squadron transitioned to B-25Ds (*left photo*) The early addition of the B-25 into RAAF service was closely connected with the Netherlands East Indies Air Force's No. 18 Squadron during the preceding two years (see "B-25s in the Dutch NEI Service," below). Of the fifty RAAF Mitchells (thirty B-25Ds and twenty B-25Js), no fewer than thirty-nine either had served with or had been allocated to No. 18 Squadron NEI before the RAAF secured them. The first twenty B-25s received in May 1944 were followed in June and July by five more B-25Ds and seven B-25Js (*right photo*). The remaining Mitchells delivered to the RAAF from Dutch allotments were five B-25Ds in August 1944 and two more B-25Js in September. The final eleven Mitchells delivered to the RAAF were B-25Js and were transferred between April and August 1945. These aircraft did not come from Dutch inventory but directly from the USAAF, but only two of them were taken on strength by No. 2 Squadron. *Both photos, AFHRC*

B-25s in Canadian (RCAF) Service

The Royal Canadian Air Force (RCAF) received 162 Mitchells, which were used mainly for training and high-altitude aerial photography sorties over uncharted areas of Canada during the war. Their use in the postwar continued; these included Mitchell IIs and IIIs in operational training and air transport roles. The RCAF retained the Mitchell until October 1963. *AFHRC*

USAAF, Soviet, Dutch, and RAF national insignia being applied at the NAA Inglewood plant during the early years of World War II. *NAA*

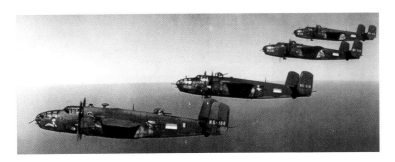

B-25s in the Dutch NEI Service

The Dutch government in exile employed the Mitchells in somewhat large numbers in combat in the Netherland East Indies (NEI) as well as in the ETO. On June 30, 1941, the Dutch contracted NAA for 162 B-25Cs and Ds (*left photo*) to be delivered to the Netherlands East Indies Air Force to meet Japanese aggression. Eventually, the first ten arrived in Australia to be used as the nucleus of the new No. 18 Squadron, operated jointly by Australian and Dutch aircrews and under Royal Australian Air Force command, flying bombing raids against Japanese targets in the East Indies for the remainder of the war. A total of 150 Mitchells were operated by the NEIAF: nineteen in 1942, sixteen in 1943, eighty-seven in 1944, and twenty-eight in 1945. During 1944, the more proficient B-25J (*right photo*) replaced most of the earlier C and D models. Following the war, B-25s were used by Dutch forces during the Indonesian National Revolution. *Both photos, AFHRC*

B-25s in Soviet Service

America supplied 862 B-25Bs, Ds, Gs, and Js (*D on left and J on right*) to the Soviet Union under Lend-Lease during World War II via the Alaska–Siberia (ALSIB) ferry route. These Mitchells totaled 10 percent of the Soviet Long-Range Aviation's (ADD) bomber fleet. During late 1942 and into 1943, B-25 aircrews generally operated as close air support for the Red Army and tactical daylight bombers attacking German railway, road, and airfield targets, but during the second half of the war, Mitchell crews also bombed targets in cities. Toward the end of the war, however, B-25s were unable to operate from short runways close to the rapidly advancing front, and many were converted into transport aircraft. B-25s that remained in Soviet air force service after the war were assigned the NATO reporting name "Bank." *Both photos, AFHRC*

B-25s in French Service

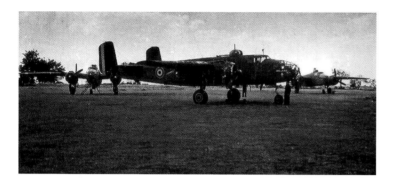

RAF No. 342 Lorraine Squadron: RAF No. 342 Lorraine Squadron was formed as part of No. 2 Group of RAF Bomber Command on April 7, 1943, with personnel from the Free French air forces transferred from the Middle East. The squadron was originally equipped with Douglas Mk IIIA Bostons, flying low-level bombing and strafing missions over France and Holland in preparation for D-day. During March and April 1945, the Bostons were replaced by Mitchell IIs, which were used for only a short time, April 9 to May 2. *AFHRC*

French Air Force GB I/20 Lorraine: Following the liberation of France and the end of the war, No. 342 Squadron transferred to the newly formed French air force (Armée de l'Air) as GB I/20 Lorraine. The Mitchell IIIs continued in operation after the war, with some being converted into fast VIP transports, and all were struck off charge in June 1947. *AFHRC*

B-25s in Chinese Service

Chinese-American Composite Wing (CACW): When the 14th Air Force was established on March 11, 1943, the CACW was created around an initial future allotment of forty B-25Cs to be supplied by Lend-Lease. By early August 1943, only enough Mitchells arrived to equip the CACW 1st and 2nd Bomb Squadrons for combat. *AFHRC*

Nationalist Chinese Air Force: Once the CBI supply chain became established, the influx of more new aircraft increased Chinese air strength, allowing the Chinese air force to gain air superiority. B-25C and D models were the first type on strength, with well over 100 B-25Cs and Ds supplied to the Nationalist Chinese, with an additional 131 B-25Js and forty-three B-25Hs supplied under Lend-Lease. Following the end of the Pacific war, four bombardment squadrons were established to fight against the Communist insurgency over China. During December 1948, the Nationalists were forced to retreat to offshore Formosa, taking many of their Mitchells with them. However, some B-25s were left behind and operated by the new People's Republic of China. *AFHRC*

B-25s in Brazilian (FAB) Service

In August 1941, Brazil became the first Latin American nation to receive the B-25 (B-25B/40-2245). During February 1942, before Brazil declared war on the Axis, six B-25Bs were sent to a training unit, but after war was declared on August 22, 1942, they were dispatched on antisubmarine patrols. However, the B-25s were ineffective long-range antisubmarine aircraft and thus were replaced, and by late August 1944, only one was airworthy. On December 18, 1943, 1 Grupo de Aviacao de Caca was formed and equipped with P-47Ds and eventually deployed to Italy with the USAAF 350th Fighter Group. With this increased commitment, Brazil requisitioned twenty-one B-25Js to fly with the P-47s in Italy, which was approved to be delivered between September and October 1944. Delivery was delayed, and no Brazilian medium-bomber unit was deployed during the war, but the FAB entered the postwar with Latin America's most powerful medium-bomber force, consisting of twenty-seven B-25s of various types. The last Brazilian B-25 was declared surplus during 1970. *AFHRC*

B-25s in Mexican (FAM) Service

Although the Mexican air force, the Fuerza Aerea Mexicana (FAM), was best known for flying the P-47 for its 201st Mexican Squadron over the Philippines, it was assigned three B-25Js under Lend-Lease during March (two) and May 1945. However, the Mitchells did not arrive until December, and since there was no Lend-Lease project number assigned to them, the aircraft were not transferred until January 1949, probably as postwar surplus sales. *AFHRC*

Postwar Mitchells

B-25 Training Versions

AT-24

During the war, the B-25 training designation was amended. The AT-24A was used to identify the first B-25 training aircraft, which were sixty stripped-down conversions of the B-25D. Subsequent B-25 conversions to the training role were the AT-24C (B-25C), AT-24B (B-25G), and the AT-24D (B-25J). The AT system was later changed, in June 1948, to a more consistent one in which the prefix and suffix letters were added on to a recognizable type number, as redesignated as the TB-25A (B-25D), TB-25C (B-25C), TB-25B (B-25G), and TB-25D (B-25J). *NAA/Rice*

TB-25J

Postwar, most of the active B-25Js were redesignated as TB-25Js, indicating that they were no longer considered as combat types. Between 1952 and 1954, the Hayes Aircraft Company, in Birmingham, Alabama, "inspected and repaired as needed" (IRAN) 979 B-25Js with various systems and equipment for training. The last US military Mitchell flight, TB-25J-25-NC (44-30854), landed at Eglin AFB on May 21, 1960. *NAA/Rice*

TB-25L

The Hayes Aircraft Company was contracted to modify seventy-five B-25Js for specialized advanced pilot training under the designation TB-25L. The aircraft were totally rebuilt, with all armament and armor removed and two passenger seats added forward of the bomb bay, and five seats were installed in the aft fuselage. TB-25s were used in the USAF's final pilot-training course at Reese AFB until January 1959, officially being withdrawn from service on May 21, 1960. *NAA/Rice*

TB-25K Fire-Control Trainer

The TB-25K was a trainer for operators of the E-1 radar fire-control system. Hughes Tool Company of Culver City, California, converted twelve B-25Js in late 1950, and succeeding contracts increased the total to 117. All military equipment was removed and an astrodome was installed above the navigator's compartment. A radome was installed forward of the transparent nose, the radar equipment instrumentation was accommodated inside a modified bomb bay, and the monitoring equipment for one instructor and the students was mounted in the aft fuselage. *NAA/Rice*

TB-25M Fire-Control Trainer

Once the TB-25K contract ended, Hughes was awarded another contract for the modification of twenty-five additional B-25Js that were modified from TB-25L aircraft. Designated as the TB-25M, these modifications were basically similar to the K model except for the installation of the more advanced E-5 fire control system, to be delivered in 1952. *NAA/Rice*

TB-24N Navigator Trainer Version

From November 1953 through December 1954, Hayes modified an additional 380 B-25Js as TB-25Ns. They were similar to the preceding TB-25Ls but were powered with R-2600-29A engines. Some were later modified as VIP transports under the designation VB-25N. Forty-seven TB-24Ns were converted to the navigator-training version by Hayes. *NAA/Rice*

CB-25J Transport Version

The USAF converted B-25J-25-NC to the CB-25J cargo/transport version, used by the Military Air Transport Service. CB-25s were used by many fighter groups in a support role. *NAA/Rice*

TB-25J Target Tow Version. *AAF*

Postwar Civilian Versions

Shortly after the end of the war, numerous surplus Mitchells were offered for sale for $8,250 cash by the Surplus Property Division of the Reconstruction Finance Corporation (RFC), which was succeeded by the War Assets Administration (WAA) in 1946. At the outset, the AAF released older B-25Cs, Ds, and Hs for disposal, retaining the newer B-25Js in active service or in storage for later use, and did not release its B-25J inventory for disposal until the late 1950s. Immediately postwar, the Navy released most of its PBJ-1 aircraft, the majority of which were B-25Js.

During 1949, NAA looked hopefully toward a potential executive transport market and modified a surplus B-25J (44-30975) into a prototype executive transport. To create more room for four more seats in the cockpit section, the forward fuselage was overhauled to make it wider and about 4 feet longer. Four more seats were added in the waist area, and the bomb bay section was reconfigured to accommodate a bunk and cargo storage. It was first flown in February 1950 under civilian registration of N5126N, but sadly, on March 1, 1950, during a cross-country tour, the aircraft crashed, killing all seven aboard. NAA's abandoned its B-25 commercial transport program several months later, the Korean War began, and NAA returned to its military aircraft roots. *NAA*

Many surplus Mitchells were employed by US Forestry Service contractors as firefighting aerial tankers that dropped fire retardant from chemical tanks installed in their bomb bays. After four crashes in the western US during the last week of July 1960, the US Forestry Service declared the Mitchell as unacceptable as an aerial tanker, and most were withdrawn from use. However, the firefighting Mitchell continued as an aerial tanker in Canada, continuing in use until 1992. Pictured is the Aerial Services B-25J that crashed during the July 1960 Magic Mountain fire, in California, killing both of the crew. *Author*

CHAPTER 2

The Flying Arsenal

Bombing Equipment and Other Ordnance

Bombardier's Compartment

The B-25 navigator, sitting in the aft radio operator / gunner's compartment, also assumed the dual bombardier role. Before the navigator could become the bombardier, the copilot had to move his seat back, fold the rudder pedals, and drop the hinged flap in the cockpit floor. The navigator would then squirm past the copilot and crawl forward into the narrow tunnel that opened under the instrument panel to the cramped bombardier's nose compartment, which was outfitted with the bombing equipment, and assume his contorted position. *MAAM*

The **Norden M-series bombsight**, located in the front of the nose, weighed 45 pounds and comprised over 2,000 parts, many of which were manufactured to minute tolerances. The Norden bombsight was a two-part system: the sight proper, and the base unit, which contained the electronics and incorporated automatic flight control equipment (AFCE). The AFCE was connected to the C-1 autopilot and allowed the bombardier to control the lateral movement of the bomber by his adjustments of the sight. The detachable upper half of the Norden contained the gyroscope for vertical stabilization of the instrument. The stabilizer consisted of the directional gyro, which was to detect deviations from the bomber's set course, and the flight gyro, which recorded any inclination for the bomber either to roll or to nose up or down. The sight was located on top of the stabilizer and was equipped with a 2.5-power telescope that was driven by a variable-speed electric motor with a gyro to keep the sight stable. *Author / AZ CAF*

Bombardier's Bombing Controls

The required controls for the bombardier in glazed-nose Mitchells were located on the port wall of the nose compartment, as part of his main control panel. In the center of this panel were the amber bomb indicator lights that informed the bombardier of the bombs present on the bomb rack stations in the bomb bay. The bomb-fusing switch on the bomb control panel simultaneously controlled the energizing of the bomb-arming controls adjacent to each bomb station and were indicted by the amber nose-fusing light. The forward panel contained the controls for bomb release sequencing. *MAAM*

Pilot's Bombing/Gun Controls

In solid-nosed Mitchells, easily reached controls enabled the pilot to release bombs from the racks either mechanically or electrically. No additional adjusting was required, since the controls, bombsight, and bomb release were preset prior to bombing. Indicator lights were included on the bomb control panel and pilot's instrument panels. *Author / Fedor Barbie III*

Bomb Bay Bombing Equipment

Bomb bay: The B-25 bomb bay, located between the flight deck and waist gunner's compartments, was equipped with bomb racks of fixed ladder-type construction designed to accommodate 100-to-l,600-pound bombs. The maximum bombload that could be carried was 6,500 pounds. A special rack could be installed to accommodate one 2,000-pound bomb. A torpedo, utilizing a special rack, could be installed under the bomb bay. A droppable bomb bay fuel tank could also be installed in the bomb bay and be released by the normal operation of the bomb controls. *AAF*

Bomb hauling: The bomb service truck was a standard 1-ton truck chassis with no cab, mounting a winch and crane that extended over the rear of the truck bed. The M5 bomb trailer was a three-wheeled, 2.5-ton-capacity vehicle used for transporting bombs from storage. It was equipped with channel irons to provide rigid seats for each bomb on the trailer, and with a chest to carry fuses, while fin posts for the bomb fins were mounted externally on these chests. The bomb lift truck for moving the finned and fused bomb under the airplane was a modified form of the common garage mechanic's hydraulic jack, with three rubber-tired wheels and a hydraulically operated platform for raising the bomb and cradle. *AAF*

Bomb Hoist

Bomb hoist: The bomb hoist assemblies were stowed under the floor of the navigator's/cannoneer's compartment, to the right side of the front entrance hatch. There were two heavily reinforced intermediate frames over the bomb bay for hoisting bombs into the bomb bay. A manhole, in the crawlway over the bomb bay, was provided for ease in stringing the bomb-hoisting cables. When bombs were being hoisted, type C-3 bomb hoist assemblies were installed in the key slots on the sides of the fuselage adjacent to the bomb bay. After B-25H-5 (43-4535), 2,000-pound bomb-carrying equipment (*shown*) was removed, since heavy bombs were used infrequently and their hoisting mechanisms required too much bomb bay area. *AAF*

Bomb bay racks: Fixed ladder-type bomb racks, one on either side of the bomb bay, were fastened to the aircraft's frames and lower longeron. The aircraft was not to be flown unless the bomb racks were installed, since they were integral structural members of the fuselage. The vertical supports or rails of the racks were made up of two aluminum channels. The bomb rails were separated by eight die-cast spacers, which constituted the bomb stations, fastened to the inside face of the bomb rails. The various bomb stations and the type of bombs to be used were printed on each spacer. The lowest bomb station was not attached to the bomb rails but was fastened to the fuselage. *Author / AZ CAF*

Bomb shackles: Two types of bomb shackles were used: the B-10 (*shown*) on the fixed bomb racks for bombs from 100 to 1,600 pounds, and the D-6 bomb shackle for the 2,000-pound bomb. Two rotating bomb support hooks at each lower end of the shackle hooked into the deadeyes (bomb support lugs) welded to the bomb casing. An interval slide bar connected to the two bomb support hooks was actuated by a lever on the top side of the shackle that fit into the release lever of the bomb release unit. A second lever that fit into the arming lever of the bomb release unit retained or released the bomb-fusing/arming wire. *Author / AZ CAF*

Wing bomb racks: The two removable wing bomb racks, attached to the undersurface of each outer wing panel, were to carry six to eight 100-to-325-pound bombs or six 325-pound Mk. 17 depth charges. The wing bomb racks were fabricated of a cast assembly that was bolted to brackets in the wing. The casting included hooks for supporting the B-7 bomb shackles and two A-2 release units with the necessary electrical and mechanical connections. The photo shows a 325-pound bomb being hoisted onto one of the removable wing racks that could attach two bombs. *AAF*

To drop bombs after the bomb door signal light illuminated, the bomb control handle was to be moved from DOORS CLOSED to the DOORS OPEN position. Then the SEL (Selective) position, to salvo all bombs at once, was chosen, or the bombardier used the intervalometer to drop the bombs in train at the selected interval. *USMC*

Bomb fusing: An armorer is shown inserting nose fuses into 100-pound GP bombs. Standard operating bomb-arming procedure was to install fuses just before takeoff, but only when the bombs were securely fixed into the aircraft. After the fuses were inserted, arming wires (*shown on two lower bombs*) were used to lock the fuse-arming mechanism in the unarmed position. When a bomb was to be released as ARMED from the rack, the wire was pulled from the fuse head, allowing the fuse vanes to rotate and arm the fuse. *AAF*

The "Kenney cocktail" was a standard M47 incendiary bomb loaded with white phosphorus that exploded spreading streamers of hotly burning phosphorous in all directions over a 150-foot diameter. Pieces of burning phosphorus could destroy vehicles, aircraft, and wooden buildings. These bombs were often dropped by the leading bombers to suppress antiaircraft (AA) fire on those aircraft following. *AAF*

Parafrag Bombs

The Parafrag was developed in the 1920s but was all but forgotten in the interwar years. Gen. George Kenney discovered 3,000 Parafrags stored in war reserve and had them shipped to Australia, where the innovative Maj. Paul "Pappy" Gunn upgraded this standard 23-pound fragmentation bomb with a special bomb tail fin unit. This tail fin unit mounted a tube on one side that contained a small parachute whose release ("rip") cord was attached on one end to the bomb bay and opened the chute upon release. The parachute slowed the bomb's descent, allowing the Mitchell to fly past the effects of the exploding bombs, thus enabling it to fly low for maximum accuracy. The official AN-M40 designation was standardized only in 1945, after the Parafrag had been in service for some time.

Parafrag attacks were flown by aircraft in a surprise, low-altitude, line-abreast formation in order to attack and leave the defending enemy AA and small-arms fire ASAP. The bomb was fused by a very sensitive proximity or instantaneous fuse that would cause it to explode several feet above the ground, spreading 800 to 1,200 pieces of fragmented bomb casing over a radius of 150 feet, devastating nearby personnel, shredding vehicles and aircraft, and exploding their fuel tanks. *AAF*

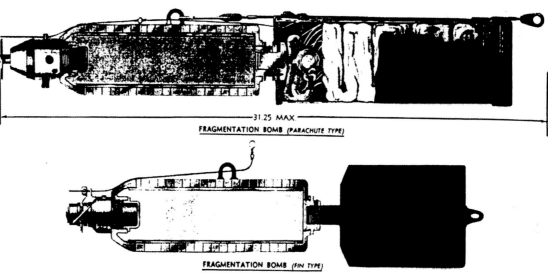

31.25 MAX

FRAGMENTATION BOMB *(PARACHUTE TYPE)*

FRAGMENTATION BOMB *(FIN TYPE)*

NAA engineers fitting a scale-model torpedo to a mahogany B-25 model for wind tunnel testing. *LoC*

While testing torpedoes in spring 1942, using B-25B "Jonah," it was found, because antishipping patrols were usually long range, that a 215- or 240-gallon self-sealing fuel tank needed to be installed above the torpedo rack in the bomb bay to increase the cruising radius of the Mitchell while carrying the torpedo. A type B-2 torpedo director operated by the pilot enabled him to approach a moving target so that a torpedo could be launched on a course to intercept the moving target. *AAF*

A 2,216-pound Mk. 13 torpedo could be mounted on B-25s as an alternate bombload; however, carrying the torpedo precluded carrying bombs except on wing racks. Torpedo-carrying equipment was not furnished with the aircraft but was available as a kit. The torpedo was mounted below the fuselage centerline on a 215-pound, aluminum, semi-external, rectangular rack, suspended through the semiclosed bomb bay door by two transverse cable slings fastened to the two lower bomb rack stations, #1 and #2. *AAF*

Depth Charges and Smoke Dispensers

Depth Charges: The B-25 was able to carry depth charges in its bomb bay: four 325 pound Mk. 17s (*shown, left photo*) or three 650-pound Mk. 29s, or on wing racks: three 325 pound Mk. 17s under each wing (*shown, right photo*). Sixty-three B-25C-25s were converted to ASW B-25G models equipped with centimetric radar, whose scanner was housed in a radome that replaced the ventral turret, a 75 mm cannon, and provisions for depth charges, but there is no record of any deployed to ASW squadrons. *Both photos, AAF*

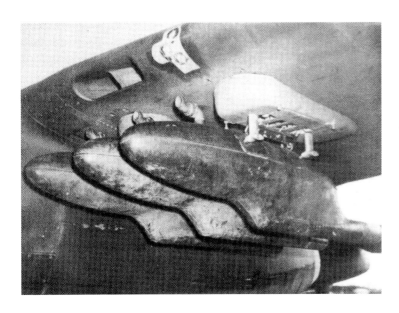

Smoke dispensers were mounted on standard wing racks and were intended to cover shipping and troops during the invasion of Pacific Islands. A similar chemical sprayer system was mounted on wing racks and in the bomb bay. *Both photos AAF*

Characteristic	4.5-inch M8	5-inch HVAR
Maximum velocity (fps)	860	1,350
Burning time (sec.)	0.20	0.88
Weight (lbs.)	38.4	136.5
HE weight (lbs.)	5.3	8.2
HE wt. as % total wt.	13.8	6.2
Diameter (in.)	4.5	5.0
Length (in.)	34	28
Total wt. of 8 rockets (lbs.)	307	1,092
Total HE wt. (lbs.)	31.8	32.8

4.5-Inch Aerial Rockets

The first combat aerial rocket was the 4.5-inch M-8 or M-10 type, which was 4.5 inches in diameter, about 3 feet long, and weighed 40 pounds. The forward (head) portion contained a nose fuse and 5 pounds of high explosive. The aft portion consisted of the motor, which contained the propellant charge. Its accurate range was about 750 yards at a maximum velocity of 865 feet per second (plus the speed of the firing aircraft). At this range the 4.5-inch rocket could penetrate 1 inch of homogenized, face-hardened steel and about 1 foot of reinforced concrete. *AAF*

As the US had no rocket designed for aircraft use, in June 1942, the AAF began to adapt rockets developed for aircraft use at the Material Center at Wright Field. US Army Ordnance had designed the M-8, 4.5-inch diameter rocket for use by ground forces as the bazooka. The first American aircraft to fire rockets (M-8s in tubular bazooka-type cluster launchers) in combat were B-25s of the 10th Air Force in Burma, in early 1944. The final report on these tests and field trials was dated February 28, 1944. It concluded that the 4.5-inch, M-8/M-10 rocket, and launcher combination was effective in frontal attacks against area targets but was not suitable for use against point targets such as armor or pillboxes due to the wide dispersion of fired rockets. *Smithsonian*

4.5-Inch Rocket Launchers

4.5-inch rockets were carried and launched from bazooka-like tubes mounted on various areas.

Underwing. *AAF*

Former 75 mm cannon tunnel and fuselage side on B-25H. *AAF*

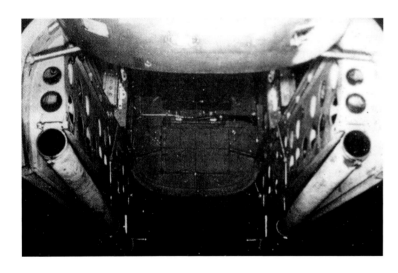

Bomb bay doors. *AAF*

5-Inch Aerial Rockets

Forward-Firing Aerial Rocket (FFAR)

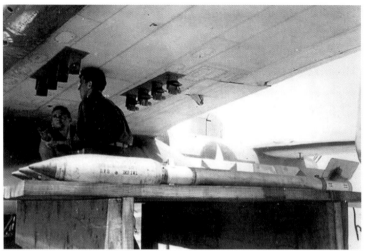

The Navy's first air-launched 5-inch forward-firing aerial rocket (FFAR), introduced in June 1943, was developed from the earlier 3.5-inch underpowered rocket motor, creating the 5-inch FFAR. *USN*

Since this FFAR was used as an aircraft-launched antisubmarine warfare (ASW) rocket, it had a 3.5-inch-diameter, nonexplosive warhead that acted by puncturing the hull, not exploding the submarine's pressure hull. When used against surface ships and land targets, an explosive 5-inch antiaircraft shell warhead was required. Performance was limited because of the increased weight, limiting speed to 485 mph. In response, the high-velocity aircraft rocket (HVAR) was developed. *USN*

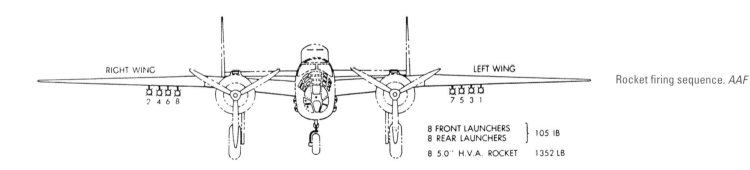

Rocket firing sequence. *AAF*

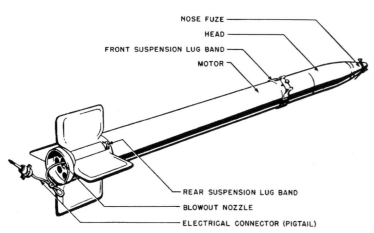

NOSE FUZE
HEAD
FRONT SUSPENSION LUG BAND
MOTOR
REAR SUSPENSION LUG BAND
BLOWOUT NOZZLE
ELECTRICAL CONNECTOR (PIGTAIL)

Figure 5–62. 5-inch High-Velocity Aircraft Rocket

The Marine PBJs were equipped with six to eight 5-inch HVAR rockets weighing approximately 1,100 pounds, on launching racks mounted outboard of each engine. The ideal release range was 1,000 yards, and the maximum effective range was 4,000 yards. The outboard rockets were fired first, beginning with the left wing and then firing those on the right wing, progressing inward until the last one, the inboard right rocket, was fired. *USN*

The high-velocity aerial rocket (HVAR) was designed at Caltech as an improvement on the FFAR, for improved accuracy from the flatter trajectory of a faster rocket. HVAR had a constant 5-inch diameter for both warhead and rocket motor, increasing propellant from 8.5 to 23.9 pounds of ballistite. Over a million "Holy Moses" HVARs were manufactured during the war, and production continued until 1955 and remained in Navy inventory until the mid-1960s. *USN*

During mid-1945, a nose-mounted internal 5-inch rocket launcher, consisting of two compact reloadable in-flight rotating drums, one on each side of the nose centerline, carrying five 5-inch spin-stabilized rockets was developed by the Naval Ordnance Test Station (NOTS), China Lake, California, and the Harvey Machine Company. *USMC*

Tiny Tim Rockets

The huge "Tiny Tim" being hoisted from a bomb carrier to an improvised carrier/loader to be attached to a Marine PBJ. *USMC*

The Tiny Tim was a new, large, high-explosive, unguided, fin-stabilized, air-to-ground rocket that was a standard 500-pound semi-armor-piercing M58A1 bomb filled with 150 pounds of TNT and attached to a steel tube equipped with a rocket motor with twenty-five nozzles producing a thrust of 37,000 pounds. The head and motor were 11.75 inches in diameter, had an overall length of 10.25 feet, and weighed about 1,275 pounds. The cruciform aluminum fins were 10 by 24 inches, attaching to two bands that were clamped around the motor when the rocket was assembled in the field. *USN*

MUNITIONS
NAVAER 00–80T–65

HEAD   MOTOR   FIN ASSEMBLY

Figure 5–53.   Head, Motor, and Fin Assembly of 11.75-inch Tiny Tim

VMB-612 Marine PBJ-1H Mitchells were equipped with the Tiny Tim rocket, but by the time they entered service, there was a lack of suitable enemy targets, which limited their deployment, and the weapon ended the war without proving its potential. *USN*

Tiny Tim's powerful rocket motor caused damage to the launching aircraft, which was solved by having the large rocket drop like a bomb on a lanyard attached to the rocket; the lanyard would sever once clear of the aircraft, causing the rocket to ignite. *USN*

Turrets, Gun Positions, Machine Guns, and Cannon

Introduction

The defensive armament of B-25s and B-25As, Bs, Cs, and many Ds was thought to be inadequate when operated as medium bombers over Europe. The first B-25 was armed with three light .30-caliber machine guns (glazed nose, dorsal, and waist) and a .50 in the tail. The C and later D models were somewhat upgraded with a fixed (C model) and flexible .50 (both guns in Ds) in the glazed nose, and two .50s in the dorsal turret, but the waist and tail armament was deleted. However, some C and Ds were very successfully configured as solid-nosed strafers in the field and led to the development of the dedicated strafer G model. The G model would mark the B-25's transition to a low-level strafer/antishipping bomber mounting two fixed .50s and fearsome 75 mm cannon in the solid nose, four .50s in blister packs mounted on the side of the fuselage, and two .50s in the dorsal turret, but there was

no waist or tail armament. The H model was a formidable strafer mounting four .50s and the 75 mm cannon in the solid nose, four .50s in blister packs, and two .50s in the dorsal turret; two .50s were mounted in the newly introduced waist and tail positions, for an awesome total of fourteen .50s and the 75 mm cannon, all augmented by eight rockets and 3,000 pounds of bombs. The final and most produced Mitchell, the J model, resumed its primary function as a medium bomber and returned to the transparent, bombardier-equipped nose armament with two fixed and one flexible .50 in the nose, and the then-standard two .50s in the dorsal turret; two .50s were in the waist and tail. However, the J's bombardier nose could be replaced at the factory by a solid nose that was equipped with eight .50s and with its maximum armament of eighteen guns.

B-25H "Barbie III," superbly restored by Jack Fedor, depicts the heavy fire power that made the B-25 the best and most feared medium bomber of World War II, mounting as many as fourteen .50s machine guns and a **75 mm** cannon, which could be supplemented by eight rockets and **3,000** pounds of bombs. *Fedor/"Barbie III"*

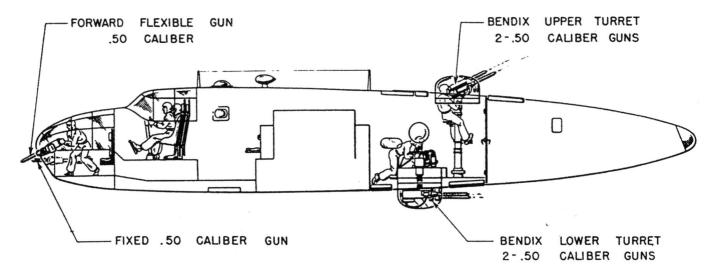

FORWARD FLEXIBLE GUN
.50 CALIBER

BENDIX UPPER TURRET
2-.50 CALIBER GUNS

FIXED .50 CALIBER GUN

BENDIX LOWER TURRET
2-.50 CALIBER GUNS

Gun Installation (Early Aircraft)

Gun Installation

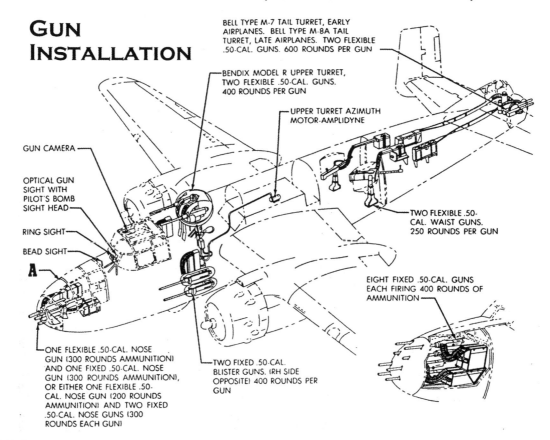

BELL TYPE M-7 TAIL TURRET, EARLY
AIRPLANES. BELL TYPE M-8A TAIL
TURRET, LATE AIRPLANES. TWO FLEXIBLE
.50-CAL. GUNS. 600 ROUNDS PER GUN

BENDIX MODEL R UPPER TURRET,
TWO FLEXIBLE .50-CAL. GUNS.
400 ROUNDS PER GUN

UPPER TURRET AZIMUTH
MOTOR-AMPLIDYNE

GUN CAMERA

OPTICAL GUN
SIGHT WITH
PILOT'S BOMB
SIGHT HEAD

RING SIGHT

BEAD SIGHT

A

TWO FLEXIBLE .50-
CAL. WAIST GUNS.
250 ROUNDS PER GUN

EIGHT FIXED .50-CAL. GUNS
EACH FIRING 400 ROUNDS OF
AMMUNITION

ONE FLEXIBLE .50-CAL. NOSE
GUN (300 ROUNDS AMMUNITION)
AND ONE FIXED .50-CAL. NOSE
GUN (300 ROUNDS AMMUNITION),
OR EITHER ONE FLEXIBLE .50-
CAL. NOSE GUN (200 ROUNDS
AMMUNITION) AND TWO FIXED
.50-CAL. NOSE GUNS (300
ROUNDS EACH GUN)

TWO FIXED .50-CAL.
BLISTER GUNS. (RH SIDE
OPPOSITE) 400 ROUNDS PER
GUN

Nose Gun Installations

Glazed Nose, Flexible Gun Position

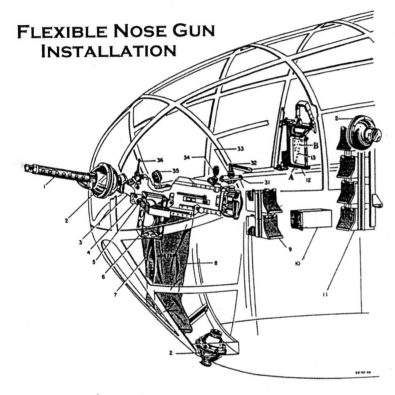

FLEXIBLE NOSE GUN
INSTALLATION

The B-25 and B-25A were equipped with a single flexible .30-caliber machine gun operated by the bombardier. This light .30-caliber gun was replaced with a heavier .50 flexible gun and a fixed gun on the B-25C-5. The flexible .50-caliber machine gun was mounted in a type K-4 ball-and-socket mount in the leading edge of the nose, directly above the bombsighting window. The gun was equipped with a type E-11 recoil adapter, a type C-19 mount adapter, an ejection chute, a link guide, a front bead sight, a rear ring sight, and a manual charging-slide assembly. The approximate firing angles of the gun were 23 degrees to either side of straight forward, 25 degrees downward, and, when the bombsight was in its operating position, 10 degrees upward. To assist in the movement of the gun were two shock cords that were suspended from the enclosure frame and attached to the recoil adapter on the gun. An ammunition belt containing 300 rounds was contained in three 100-round boxes strapped together on a shelf on the right side of the compartment. *Both photos, author / AZ CAF*

Glazed Nose, Fixed Gun Installation

FIXED NOSE GUN INSTALLATION

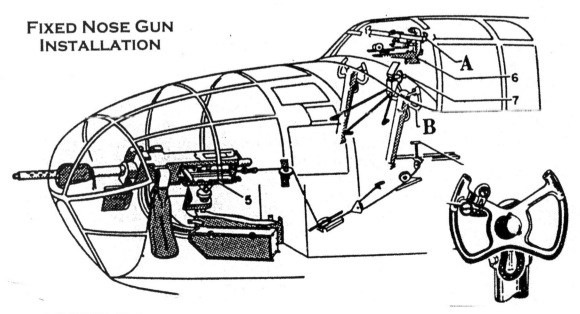

One fixed .50-caliber machine gun was mounted on the right side of the bombardier's compartment below the flexible gun ammunition box shelf. A 300-round ammunition box was held to the aft right side of the compartment floor by quick-release latches, which permitted the easy removal of the box for loading ammunition. A flexible chute fed the ammunition belt from the box to the gun. Ejected shell cases passed through the metal ejection chute aft into a cloth bag, which was attached by dot fasteners to the ammunition box and the right side of the compartment. Ejected links were caught in a zippered cloth bag attached to the inboard side of the gun. When two fixed nose guns were installed, only 275 rounds per gun were carried. Initially, all guns were manually charged in flight by the bombardier. *Both photos, author / AZ CAF*

Pappy Gunn's Early B-25C/D Strafers

The forty-three-year-old Paul Gunn was given the nickname "Pappy" by the much-younger fliers he served with in World War II. Because of his successful armament modifications of A-20 Havoc light bombers, Gen. George Kenney ordered Gunn to modify B-25s by adding more forward-firing machine guns onto each aircraft. A squadron was equipped in time to perform effective service in the February 1943 Battle of the Bismarck Sea. Gunn, promoted to major, was sent back to the United States to oversee North American Aviation's factory production of B-25s with the added strafing guns and a forward-firing 75 mm cannon in their noses. *AAF*

Paul "Pappy" Gunn and Jack Fox collaborated to reconfigure a B-25C/D prototype modification named "Pappy's Folly" to replace the standard bombardier nose with four .50-caliber machine guns, each protruding through the standard glazed nose and fed by 500-round boxes. From Gunn's work during the war, the B-25 would prove to be the most compliant American aircraft to the numerous field and depot modifications demanded of it, and the Gunn/Fox strafer modifications would directly influence future B-25G and H design and production. *AAF*

B-25C Mitchell, #41-12443, nicknamed "Mortimer," with the standard C model nose being prepared to become a strafer at an Australian depot. The right photo shows the conversion, with the glazing painted over opaque and the four .50s protruding from the lower nose. Four .50s located in two blister packs gave the conversion a potent array of eight forward-firing machine guns. *AAF*

SOLID NOSE EIGHT GUN INSTALLATION

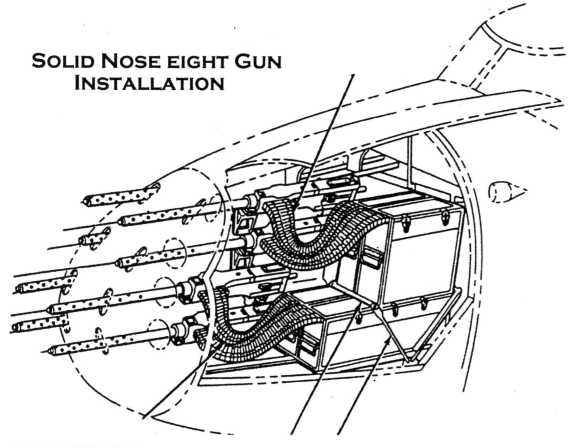

The success of the B-25C/D strafer modifications led to the B-25G, which was a dedicated factory-built strafer that was succeeded by the more efficient B-25H strafer. However, the solid-nosed B-25J, equipped with eight nose .50s, gave it a maximum armament of eighteen guns, made the solid-nosed B-25J the most heavily armed attack aircraft in the Allied arsenal. Sometimes, the package guns on the sides of the J fuselage were deleted, with the remaining fourteen guns considered being more than enough forward-directed firepower. *Photos 1 and 2, AAF; photo 3, USN*

Solid-Nose, Fixed-Gun B-25 G and H Strafer

B-24G, H, and J solid-metal noses formed a compartment for the four to eight .50-caliber nose guns and ammunition boxes. The lower nose section was fixed and provided for a cannon blast tube and a cannon muzzle close-off assembly. For the four-gun installation, the upper portion of the nose was a hinged hood that could be swung open for gaining access to the guns and boxes. For the eight-gun installation, the hood opened on both sides of the nose. Each gun, mounted on a front mount and a rear post, was equipped with a solenoid, a charging slide assembly, a link guide, a barrel-opening close-off cover, and quick-release attachments for the ammunition chute. The guns were charged and fired by the pilot. The ammunition belts were fed from the boxes to the guns through flexible feed chutes, and the ejected cases and links passed downward to the case and linked container beneath the boxes. Later, some four-gun/cannon-equipped strafers had their cannons deleted, and two additional .50s were installed in the former cannon area and orifice (*pictured left*). Left: AAF; right: USN

SOLID NOSE GUN INSTALLATION

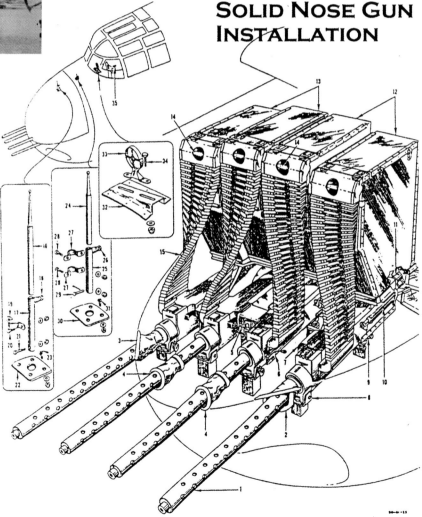

During July 1943, B-25C "Dirty Dora" (41-12971) of the 345th Bomb Group was modified at the Townsville, Australia, 4th Air Depot into a four–nose gun strafer variant. After flying 175 combat missions, this B-25 was declared war-weary during August 1944. *AAF*

This J model of the 490th Bomb Squadron, 341st Bomb Group, had been field-converted to a six-gun configuration directly through the glazed nose. The group's Mitchells served in the CBI from September 1942 to November 1945. *AAF*

"Reina del Pacifico" (43-36020) of the 501st Bomb Squadron, 345th Bomb Group, was field-converted to an unusual five-gun nose configuration. *AAF*

This B-25D-1 (41-30276), formerly "Sir Beetle," of the 498th Bomb Squadron, 345th Bomb Group, was declared war-weary and placed in the Biak dump, where it was salvaged by Capt. Victor Tatelman. The B-25 had its nose section replaced with a B-25J eight–nose gun configuration, and the overhauled B-25 was nicknamed "Dirty Dora II," after Tatelman's former B-25C "Dirty Dora" (*shown above*). *AAF*

The AAF was looking to develop a ground attack bomber to replace the Douglas A-20, but the estimated development time to bring this concept to fruition would have been at least a year (i.e., the Beech XB-38), but the AAC needed an immediate remedy, and that was the B-25. For testing, B-25C-1-NA (41-13296) (*pictured*) was modified to the XB-25G standard. After successful testing, NAA received an AAF contract for 400 cannon-equipped B-25G-5 and -10s (without lower turrets), which were delivered between May and August 1943. Although the cannon-carrying B-25G was not as successful in combat as anticipated, NAA received an order for an additional 1,000 B-25H attack strafers, which carried the lighter-weight 75 mm cannon and four nose guns (vs. two). *NAA/Rice*

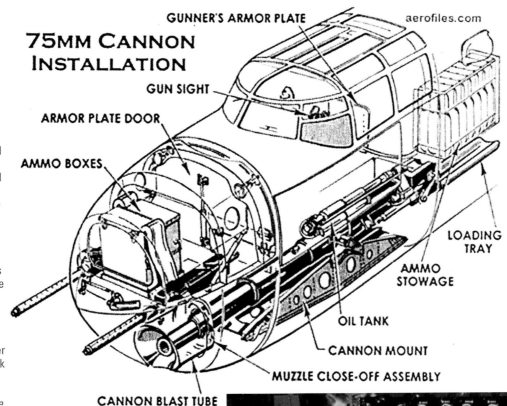

75MM CANNON INSTALLATION

aerofiles.com

GUNNER'S ARMOR PLATE

GUN SIGHT

ARMOR PLATE DOOR

AMMO BOXES

LOADING TRAY

AMMO STOWAGE

OIL TANK

CANNON MOUNT

MUZZLE CLOSE-OFF ASSEMBLY

CANNON BLAST TUBE

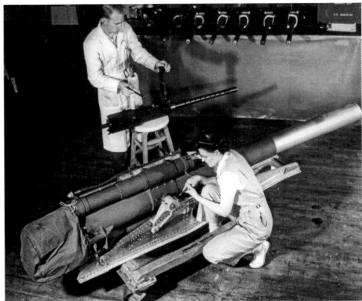

The Mitchell's 75 mm cannon assembly (cannon and ammunition) was 9 feet, 6 inches long and weighed 1,296 pounds. Up to the end of World War II, the 75 mm cannon of the B-25G/H was the second-largest gun equipping any aircraft, exceeded in size only by the 105 mm cannon experimentally equipped on the Italian Piaggio P.108A. In the postwar the B-25's 75 mm cannon was exceeded by the 105 mm howitzer carried by the Lockheed AC-130 Spectre gunship. This PR photo was designed to show a .50-caliber machine gun compared to the 75 mm cannon. *NAA/AAF*

The former bombardier glazed nose was replaced with an armored solid nose shortened by the aerodynamic maximum of 26 inches, which reduced the bomber's overall length to 51 feet. The end of the cannon barrel remained just inside the nose contour, which was strengthened so it could withstand prolonged firing of the heavy 75 mm rounds. The cannon was augmented by two side-by-side .50s mounted in the nose, which were intended to be used as antiflak weapons and for ranging purposes in the sighting of the cannon. Both the cannon and the nose guns were aimed by the pilot, using a type N-3B optical gunsight fired by the pilot by pressing the trigger under the left-hand side of the control wheel. *Author / Fedor Barbie III*

The bombardier's crawl tunnel in the lower left-hand side of the nose was the ideal location for the cannon, which was 9 feet, 6 inches long, since it provided enough room for the cannon and its recoil along with space in the navigator's compartment for ammunition storage. The cannon was mounted in a cradle that extended under the pilot's seat. Because the bomber was more exposed to enemy fire on its attacks, additional armor was installed in the nose and cockpit area. Its recoil mount (for the 21-inch recoil) and the cannon mount assembly were bolted to the floor in the tunnel beneath the left side of the pilot's compartment. The breech extended aft to the left forward side of the cannoneer's compartment for manual loading of the large shell. *Author / Fedor Barbie III*

Rather than bear the extra weight, high cost, and protracted development time of an autoloader, the 75 mm rounds were manually loaded into the cannon breech (*shown*) by the navigator/cannoneer, who was provided with a folding seat, a cannon recoil foot guard, a leg strap, a wooden loading ram, and an ammunition loading tray attached to the cannon breech ring. After takeoff the cannoneer would manually charge the blister guns and cannon. The cannon ammunition stowage rack, a box protected on three sides by armor plate, was installed on the navigator's shelf (*shown*) directly above the cannon breech. The ammunition rack contained an upper rack and a lower rack, which together provided for seven vertical stowage sections, with each section stowing three rounds, totaling twenty-one rounds. *AAF*

The 75 mm cannon shell was equivalent to seventy-eight .50-caliber machine gun bullets. *Author / Barbie III*

The 75 mm projectile was 26 inches long, was 3 inches in diameter, and weighed 20 pounds (equivalent to seventy-eight .50-caliber bullets), of which 15 pounds made up the projectile, which contained 1.5 pounds of TNT. After the projectile was fired, a spent shell case was ejected from the recoiling cannon against a shell deflector that sent the case down a chute and overboard. The cannon's relatively low 1,930-feet-per-second muzzle velocity gave the shell a relatively low trajectory, making accurate range determination and trajectory essential and requiring a straight run in to the target, which increased the attacking Mitchell's vulnerability to enemy fire. The cannon was accurate, but usually no more than four rounds could be loaded and fired during an attack. *NAA*

An interesting photo of an armorer cleaning the bore of a 75 mm cannon mounted on a rather lightly armed 345th Bomb Group B-25H, "Pride of the Yankees." The bomber has only two nose .50s and no blister packs. *AAF*

Cannon-armed B-25Hs offered no particular advantage over specially adapted strafers armed exclusively with multiple forward-firing machine guns at this stage in the war, since targets specifically suited for cannon attack were relatively scarce, and many targets that were vulnerable to the cannon were also vulnerable to a battery of .50-inch machine guns or to bombs. Consequently, the use of the heavy cannon was generally abandoned in the Southwest Pacific by August 1944. *Painting by Roy Grinnell*

75 mm Cannon Installation

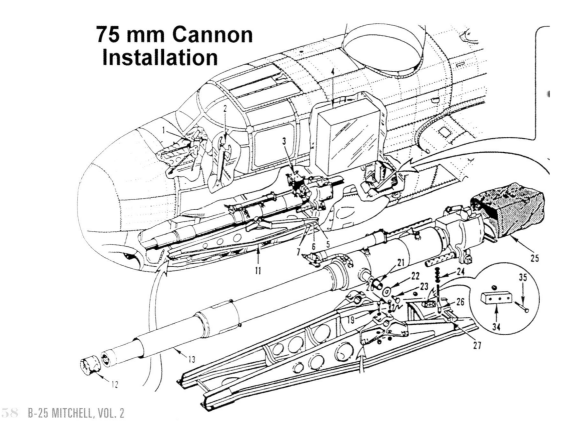

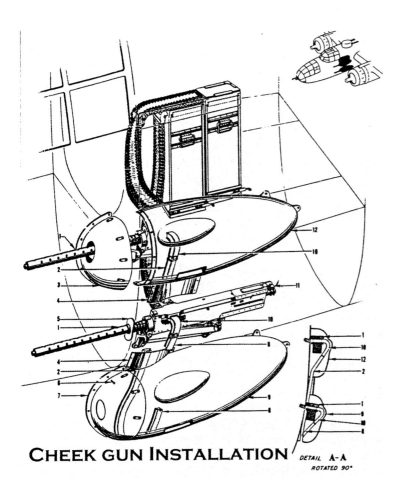

CHEEK GUN INSTALLATION

DETAIL A-A
ROTATED 90°

In mid-1943 the cannon-equipped B-25Gs arrived in the Southwest Pacific Area (SWPA) and were tested by Maj. Paul Gunn from mid-November through December. Gunn was mostly pleased with the 75 mm cannon, but he recommended that the G model needed the addition of forward-firing .50-caliber machine guns. The Service Command began a wide-ranging armament modification program running from November 1943 to April 1944, to add to the Mitchell's forward firepower, specifically developing the fuselage gun pack for the H and J models. The photo pictures an early primitive blister pack fabricated in the SWPA. Note the very crude, narrow blast plates adjacent to the gun barrels. Although their appearance was slightly different, there was an available field modification to add side blister guns to nearly any B-25 model that was not manufactured with them. *AAF*

The fuselage gun packs (NAA company nomenclature) were also called "cheek packs" and, most commonly, "blister packs" in the field. There were many different styles of cheek gun pack housings, but they were generally faired, rectangular, or long oval metal pods fastened to the fuselage and accessed via a downward-opening, hinged cover door. The pack enclosed two .50-caliber machine guns that were anchored to the fuselage by a reinforced plate. The barrel of the top gun was usually staggered slightly behind that of the lower gun. The ammunition boxes, supported on a shelf structure at the right side of the cannoneer/navigator's compartment, were loaded with approximately 400 rounds of belted ammunition that moved along flexible chutes to feed the guns. The cannoneer/navigator charged the blister guns in flight by pulling out and releasing the charging handles. The pilot fired these guns simultaneously with a red firing button located on the control column wheel spokes. *Author / AZ CAF*

It was found that the muzzle blast from these guns could pop fuselage rivets and cause damage to the thin aluminum fuselage skin and the surrounding areas. The employment of bronze phosphor blast arrestors (*shown*) and the attachment of large sheet-metal plates to the fuselage blast area at the end of the muzzle (*shown*) remedied the situation. *Author / AZ CAF*

Bendix Model A Dorsal Turrets

The all-electric Bendix dorsal turret was used exclusively on the B-25, beginning with the B-25B. Initially, the original all-electric Bendix Model A dorsal turret was to be armed with two light, twin, .30-caliber machine guns incorporated to AAC standards exclusively in the B-25 in the late 1930s, beginning with the B-25B. The first Bendix Model A dorsal turret (250CE-3), armed with twin .50s, was located in the aft fuselage compartment behind the bomb bay, replacing the single, flexible, dorsal .30-caliber machine gun on the B-25 and B-25A that fired through an enclosed hatch. *AAF*

The early Bendix Model A dorsal turrets encountered numerous electrical-system malfunctions, virtually impossible smooth tracking of a target, jammed guns, and poor turret sealing, causing either cold drafts or the sucking of warm air from the cabin. They were designed without consideration for the gunner's size, wearing full flying gear, and he became uncomfortably jammed behind the twin guns and the back edge of the turret. The Bendix Model A dorsal turret's aft location was continued on the B-25C/D and G models. *AAF*

The RAF Mitchell III was equipped with an Emerson dorsal turret while the Mitchell II was fitted with the Martin-built dorsal turret. *NAA/Rice*

Bendix Model R Dorsal Turrets

FORWARD BENDIX DORSAL TURRET LOATION B-25H

34 380

BENDIX MODEL R DORSAL TURRET

After the Bendix ventral turret was canceled during its production run, and waist guns and tail guns were added at modification depots or in the field to alleviate this armament deficiency, the dorsal turret had to be moved forward in its Bendix Model R configuration (250CE-4) to a position forward in the navigator's compartment, just behind the cockpit, which helped maintain the proper center of gravity to balance the weight added to the rear by the waist guns and tail turret.

Basically, the Model R was an improved version of the Model A. The upper visible portion of the turret consisted of the guns, control housing, center column, radial support, and Plexiglas canopy. *Author / Fedor Barbie III*

02344

The all-electric Bendix dorsal turret was used exclusively on the B-25, beginning with the B-25B. The original B-25 design incorporated the late 1930s AAC standards utilizing the light .30-caliber machine gun in five flexible hand-held positions: one in the nose, one each in the ventral and dorsal rear fuselage, and two in the waist position. The Bendix Model A dorsal turret was located in aft fuselage compartment behind the bomb bay, replacing the single flexible dorsal .30-caliber machine gun on the B-25 and B-25A that fired through a enclosed hatch. *AAF*

BENDIX MODEL R DORSAL TURRET

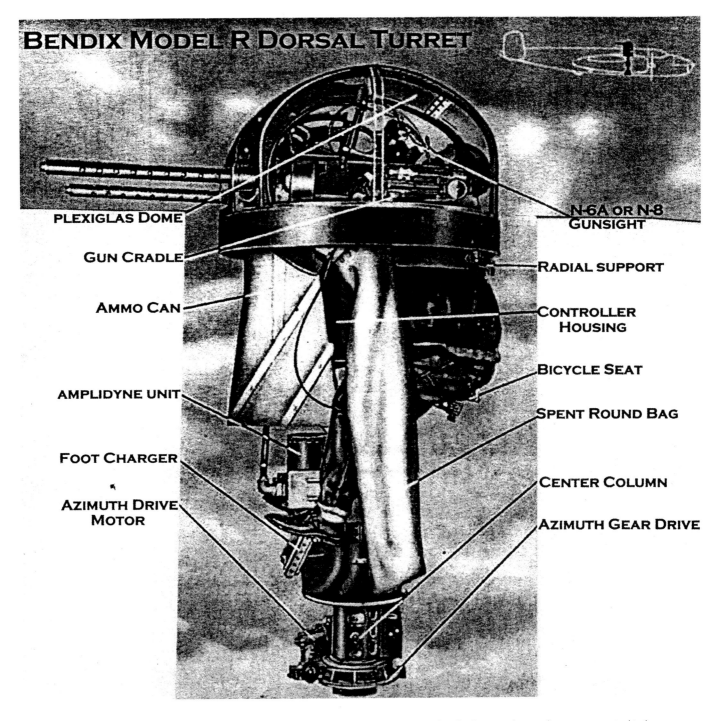

PLEXIGLAS DOME

GUN CRADLE

AMMO CAN

AMPLIDYNE UNIT

FOOT CHARGER

AZIMUTH DRIVE MOTOR

N-6A OR N-8 GUNSIGHT

RADIAL SUPPORT

CONTROLLER HOUSING

BICYCLE SEAT

SPENT ROUND BAG

CENTER COLUMN

AZIMUTH GEAR DRIVE

The Model R was electrically powered from the bomber's central control system, mounted twin .50-caliber M-2 machine guns that were aimed by an N-6A or N-8 gunsight, and was equipped with upgraded recoil-absorbing mechanisms, firing solenoids, and foot chargers. Each gun was equipped with an Edgewater recoil adapter, a type G-11 firing solenoid, a manual charging slide, and case and link ejection chutes. The photo view is looking aft from the navigator's station. *Author / Fedor Barbie III*

TURRET PEDESTAL

The dorsal turret was installed on a support pedestal bolted to the floor, while the upper part of the turret was guided by rollers that rode in a bearing race installed in the top of the fuselage. The gunner sat on an adjustable, downward-latching bicycle seat and placed his feet on adjustable foot rests that revolved with the turret; his head and shoulders were located between the guns, and his feet were supported on adjustable gun-charging footrests. The footrests were adjusted to the gunner's height by moving them up or down in the notches on the foot slide. *Author / Fedor Barbie III*

The turret's gun controls turned the guns "as you would steer a bicycle." To raise the guns, the heels of the handle were pressed down and pulled up to depress them. The guns were supplied by two large ammunition boxes marked "Right (gun)" and "Left (gun)," which carried 400–440 rpg. Ammunition belts and chutes were arranged to furnish a continuous ammunition supply to the guns. *Author / Fedor Barbie III*

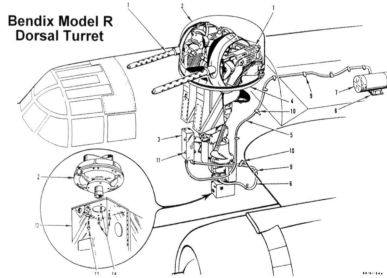

Bendix Model R Dorsal Turret

The turret was designed to protect the bomber's upper hemisphere, and the canopy permitted the gunner to have an unrestricted view in that hemisphere. The turret controls (*pictured*) rotated the guns 360 degrees, full circle, in azimuth and swung from horizontal 0 degrees to a nearly vertical 82 degrees to 8 degrees zenith (up). The speed of the turret could be varied from ¼ degree to 12 degrees per second in low speed and from ¼ degree to thirty-three degrees per second in high speed. *Author / AZ CAF*

The guns were equipped with firing cutouts and electric dynamic brakes that prevented the guns from firing aft into the vertical stabilizers and forward into the propellers and fuselage just forward of the turret. Two small angled fairings (*bottom of photo*) were added on top of the fuselage just aft of the gun muzzles when the dorsal turret was in the stowed position pointing aft. These fairings were actually ½-inch pieces of steel armor that deflected accidental "cooked off" bullets away from the tail gunner's position when the turret was in the stowed position. *MAAM*

Bendix Model K Ventral Turret

The Bendix Model K amplidyne ventral turret, placed in B-25 Cs and Ds (and B-24Ds), was a 392-pound, solid retractable turret designed around a central column and 300 pounds of guns and ammunition. This turret was retracted into the fuselage belly when not in use, the gun barrels fitting into slots in the fuselage when the turret was in the fully up position. It mounted twin .50-caliber machine guns fed by 390 rounds of ammunition per gun from ammunition boxes bolted to the lower canopy. The empty shell cases and links were ejected overboard through ejection chutes. Observation windows were cut into the fuselage just above the floor level on each side of the turret. The ventral turret provided defensive protection for the aft and side and the lower forward area except where the gunfire was restricted. The guns were sighted by a complex periscope system of lenses and mirrors mounted on top of the turret's center column. A kneeling gunner aimed the guns by looking through the periscope sight eyepiece and directed the guns by operating a dual hand control. The optical sighting system was cumbersome and difficult for gunners to use, and hydraulic fluid and dust and mud tended to blur the system when operating from unimproved airfields. The gunner was confined in an uncomfortable kneeling position and, while looking through the periscope, was unable to see his hands or the twin gun barrels. The gunner could become dizzy, disoriented, and even nauseated when tracking enemy fighters through this sight. Furthermore, the turret required almost a minute to be lowered into place and set up for firing. The retractable ventral turret was generally disliked by the Mitchell crews and was often removed in the field, eliminating 700 pounds and affording space for a long-range fuel tank. This turret had a comparatively short AAF service life and was discontinued during production of the B-25G-5 from aircraft 42-65001 onward.

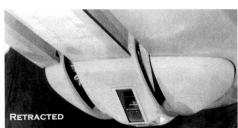

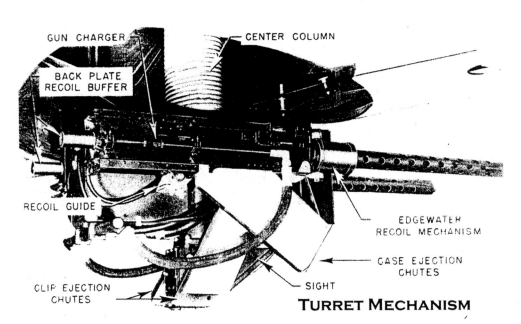

TURRET MECHANISM

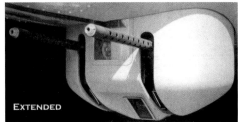

Both photos, AAF

Early Waist Windows

The B-25 and B-25A were provided with two opposing open waist gun positions in the rear fuselage, each mounting a light .30-caliber machine gun. For combat firing, the gun had to be lifted from its stowage position in front of the waist window and inserted into its ball-and-socket mount, with the barrel extending out of the window's lower rear corner. It would appear that NAA finalized the design of these waist windows some time before the B-25H factory-provided waist windows appeared, since many conversion kits were shipped to modification centers to upgrade the armament of the B-25C/Ds. These modifications on the C/D models became somewhat common in some squadrons, although the midfuselage position of the dorsal turret meant that the dorsal turret gunner's feet must have been very close to the waist gunner's head as the turret rotated. *AAF*

Another crude SWPA waist field modification. *AAF*

After the ventral turret was discontinued during B-25G-5 production, some B-25Gs from B-25G 42-65001 onward had postproduction, jury-rigged waist positions and a single tail guns added at modification depots to improve their defensive armament. *AAF*

Later Factory-Provided B-25H Waist Positions

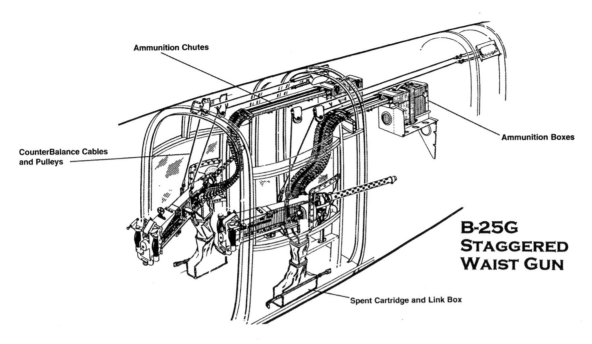

Ammunition Chutes

Ammunition Boxes

CounterBalance Cables
and Pulleys

**B-25G
STAGGERED
WAIST GUN**

Spent Cartridge and Link Box

The movement of the Bendix dorsal turret forward opened up the rear fuselage compartment to provide for the first factory-furnished, opposing, flexible, .50-caliber waist gun positions, which appeared on the B-25H. Waist defense was improved by installing large, enclosed, cylindrically shaped, convex "bay windows" cut into the fuselage on both sides aft of the wing. The windows were staggered to allow more room for the gunners to operate and not get in each other's way. The window on the port side was placed slightly farther aft from the rear of the wing than that on the starboard side, which had its forward vertical frame a few inches away from the wing flaps. Each flexible .50 barrel projected through a sealing canvas boot around the barrel located in the lower aft corner of each window. The *Flight Manual* warned: "As there are no fire cutout provisions on waist guns, be careful not to fire into the tail or nacelle." *Both photos and drawing, AAF*

The gun was released from its stowage position by pushing a plunger located on the aft end of the gun adapter. It was charged by pulling back and releasing the charging handle, and then the safety was moved to FIRE. Bungee cables facilitated maneuvering the guns during firing. While riding, the gunners were provided folding seats forward of the turret windows.

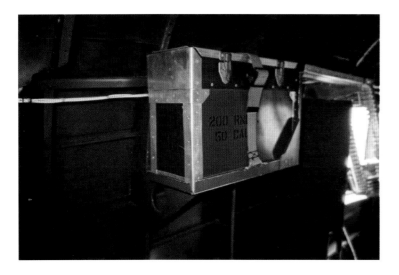

Two hundred rounds of ammunition were fed to each gun from an overhead box per gun, located on storage shelves aft of the gun via belts passing through the fixed and flexible stainless-steel feed chutes. *All photos, author / Fedor Barbie III*

Each gun was mounted on a Bell E-11 trunnion yoke recoil adapter and was equipped with a manual charging handle and slide, a feed chute attachment, a link ejection chute, a ring-and-bead sight or an electric N-8 or N-8A optical sight, a link guide, and a canvas case and link container. After firing, the safety was moved to SAFE, and the gun was stowed by a latch when not in use.

Original Tail Guns

North American demonstration of its first Mitchell tail gun position with employee/gunner positioned behind .50-caliber machine gun and clam shell doors. *NAA*

The original B-25 .50-caliber tail gun position was eliminated and was greatly reduced in size to become little more than a prone observation post, being terminated at its extreme end with a transparent, clear view cap. This tail configuration remained in effect for the B, C, and early D models, although some of these had the tail cone removed and a single .30 or .50 tail gun added in the field, in which the gunner had to lie prone, which limited the gun's field of fire. *AAF*

The earliest B-25 cone-shaped tail turret mounted a flexible .50-caliber machine gun, the only .50-caliber gun among five .30-caliber guns in the nose (1), dorsal (1), ventral, and waist (2) positions. The gun opened through clamshell Plexiglas doors that were similar to those pioneered by the Douglas B-23 Dragon. The gunner sat on a metal chair mounted close to the floor, with the gun between his bent legs while he looked through a sighting system. *AAF*

After the ineffective ventral turret was removed, leaving only the dorsal turret for defense, a few late B-25D and more G models were equipped with a dedicated tail gun position mounting a single .50-caliber gun installed at the factory and modification centers. The gunner kneeled to fire the gun by using a ring-and-bead gunsight. These positions closely resembled the twin .50s installation that would become standard on later on B-25 H and J models. *AAF*

B-25H and J Tail Turret with the Bell Gun Mount Assembly

The B-25H and J models were the first Mitchells to have a factory-supplied tail turret, which required a deepening of the rear fuselage by 7 inches with a canvas boot or slotted metal fairing enclosing the twin gun barrels. *Author / AZ CAF*

The gunner sat on a low, cushioned, stool-type seat supported on a floor-mounted pedestal located behind the armor plate. The gunner was instructed to never remain on the seat during takeoffs or landings, during quick changes in speed, and at "times that make the tail an extremely dangerous place to be." The controls were like those of any "ordinary" turret, with the adapter's hydraulic power system allowing the gunner to "easily and firmly" swing the guns and sight. The control housing, handles, and hydraulic pump and motor unit were located on the armor plate in front of him. *Author / AZ CAF*

The streamlined turret had three windows on each side, a removable top hatch that could be jettisoned for an emergency bailout (the aft fuselage hatch was used in a controlled bailout), and a flat, rear-facing armored glass window in front of the gunsight. *AAF*

Close up of tail gunner "cockpit" with long plexiglas escape hatch overhead. *AAF*

The Bell gun mount assembly, called the Bell adapter, was a power-driven flexible gun mount developed to increase the firepower of the tail gun position in the B-25 (the type M-7) and B-26 (the type M-6A), with the only difference between the two being in the mounting bracket. The Bell adapter was powered in elevation and azimuth by pressure in a closed hydraulic system developed by a constant-speed electric motor. The guns had a 38-degree traverse in either direction from the longitudinal centerline, and a vertical movement of 45 degrees above horizontal and 35 degrees below horizontal. The Bell adapter was equipped with a twin-gun adapter that mounted two .50-caliber type M-2 pistol-grip machine guns sighted by a type N-8 or N-6A gunsight (later variants were equipped with the revolutionary K-10 computing sight). The long, twisted ammo feed chute assembly was loaded with approximately 300 rounds for each gun, by passing the double loop ends aft through chutes and booster motors to the guns. The loaded ammunition boxes located in the aft fuselage behind the turret were installed on the shelves, ready for loading into the guns. *Drawing, AAF; photo, author / AZ CAF*

Gun Fume Venting

The air outlet for the cannoneer's compartment was located on the left side of the compartment below the cannoneer's shelf and exited on the lower port fuselage near the cannon breech. *Author / Fedor Barbie III*

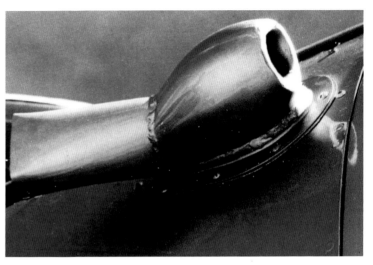

The outlets for the nose gun compartment were located beneath each machine gun and on the starboard side of the bombardier's glazed or solid nose compartment. Both duct outlets could be opened or closed by the occupant of the compartment, with the position of the control being indicated by a nameplate on each control. The outlets in the nose gun compartment were opened and closed from a control in the pilot's compartment, which operated a butterfly valve in the nose gun compartment duct. *Author / AZ CAF*

Or just open a window. *AAF*

Gun-Opening Sealing

In early B-25s the drafts entering the gun openings to the outside could be uncomfortable in European skies. Fortunately, the Mitchell was a low-altitude attacker over North Africa and then in the tropical South Pacific. These photos demonstrate the sealing measures around gun orifices.

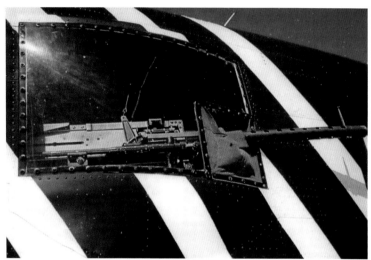

While B-17 gunners suffered the intense cold greatly when flying during their bomber's high-altitude bombing missions, B-25 waist gunners often could be too warm manning their positions in the tropical South Pacific heat and humidity. *Author / Fedor Barbie III*

Any glazed bomber nose always had a notoriously drafty reputation, but fortunately the Mitchell bombardier rode inside the fuselage when not on bombing runs or manning the flexible guns. *MAAM*

Instead of a prefabricated metal fairing covering the truncated tail turret of the Bell gun mount assembly, a simple canvas covering was attached over the rear fuselage opening. *Author / Fedor Barbie III*

Armor Protection

The B-25A introduced the basic armor protection for the crew, which was to be augmented in forthcoming models with additional armor and modifications introduced on the B-25G/H and B-25J models. *AAF*

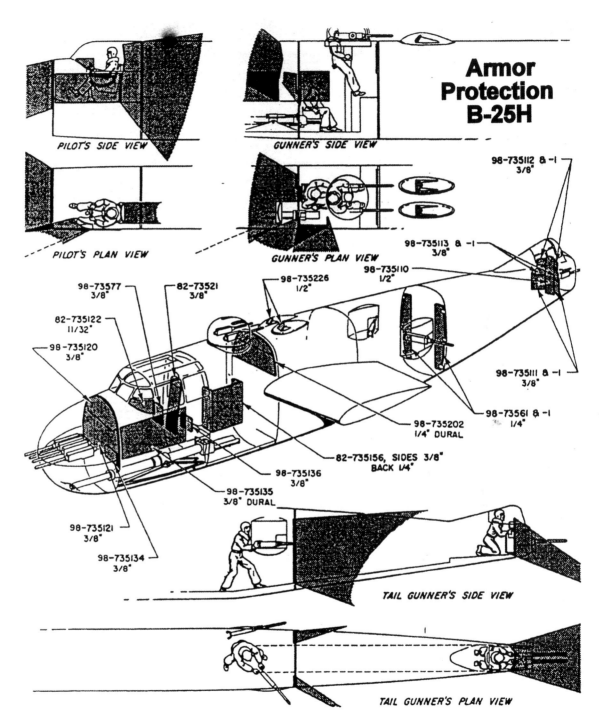

PILOT'S SIDE VIEW

GUNNER'S SIDE VIEW

Armor Protection B-25H

PILOT'S PLAN VIEW

GUNNER'S PLAN VIEW

98-735112 & -1
3/8"

98-735113 & -1
3/8"

98-735110
1/2"

98-735111 & -1
3/8"

98-73561 & -1
1/4"

98-73577
3/8"

82-73521
3/8"

98-735226
1/2"

82-735122
11/32"

98-735120
3/8"

98-735202
1/4" DURAL

82-735156, SIDES 3/8"
BACK 1/4"

98-735136
3/8"

98-735135
3/8" DURAL

98-735121
3/8"

98-735134
3/8"

TAIL GUNNER'S SIDE VIEW

TAIL GUNNER'S PLAN VIEW

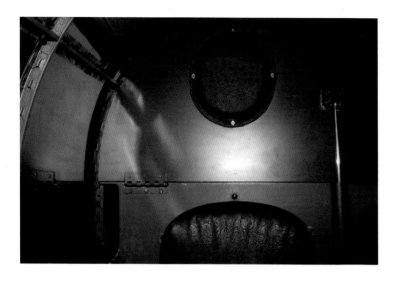

The bombardier was provided with a riding seat that had a 3/8-inch armor back and seat plate. Additional armor protection was provided on the B-25J nose floor for the bombardier. *Author / Fedor Barbie III*

A large, rectangular, external flak plate was installed below the pilot's cockpit on the left-hand side of the B-26H, protecting the pilot and instruments. *Author / Fedor Barbie III*

The two pilots' bucket seats were backed by a full-length, 3/8-inch plate. The B-25J-25 production block introduced new types of armored seats for both pilots, dubbed "coffin seats" because they enclosed the pilots in 145 pounds of armor protection. The seat and back were 5/16-inch steel armor, while a sheath of 3/8-inch Alcad wrapped around the pilots, from one side over their heads and to the opposite side. *Author / Fedor Barbie III*

Armor plate was installed just aft of the tail gunner's seat and gun controls. *MAAM*

Test Firing and Combat Training

After being boresighted and with wheels chocked, a new B-25J from the Kansas City factory test-fired its awesome fourteen frontal .50-caliber machine gun array. A 27-by-37-foot concrete, sand-filled bunker was built into a Missouri River levee for the testing. After firing at least twenty-five rounds through each gun, they were removed, cleaned, wrapped, and stowed in the fuselage before delivery. The bunker sand had to be replaced every two weeks, since the lead from the fired bullets was pulverized. *AAF*

Officially designated as the AAF Temporary Building (Target) T-799 Japanese battleship, but called the *Muroc Maru*, it was a 650-foot-long, life-size mockup replica of a Japanese heavy cruiser that was built at Muroc/Rogers Dry Lake, California. It was constructed for the then-large sum of $35,820 of 4 × 4s and chicken wire covered with tar paper and chicken feathers, but due to the strong desert winds and temperature extremes, the chicken feather feature was soon abandoned. Sand berms were constructed around the *Muroc Maru* to simulate a ship's bow wave and wake. On very hot days, mirages would give the appearance of the *Muroc Maru* sailing at sea. *AAF*

The *Maru* was variously for target and bombing practice, strafing practice, and target identification training. The structure remained in use for training until 1950, when it was declared a hazard to air navigation and disassembled following the dangerous clearance of unexploded ordnance. *AAF*

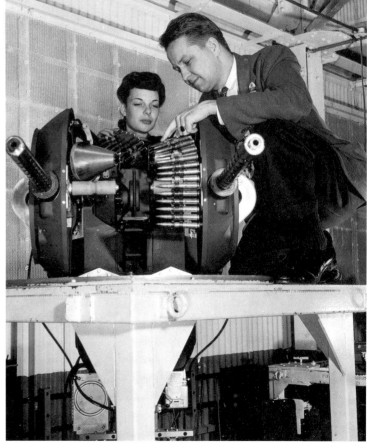

Bendix publicity photo showing a female worker the dorsal gun turret as the result of her labors. *Bendix*

Mitchells in Action

After making its low-level attack, a 345th Bomb Group B-25 strafer leaves Simpson Harbor, Rabaul, which was crowded with Japanese shipping. *AAF*

A dramatic photo of the B-25J nicknamed "Jaunty Jo" (43-3692), of the 498th Bomb Squadron, 345th Bomb Group, shown receiving a fatal AA hit over the Byoritsu Refinery, Formosa. *AAF*

Photo sequence of a Japanese destroyer under attack by a 345th Bomb Group strafer off New Hanover Island, on February 16, 1944. *AAF*

CHAPTER 3

Mitchell Machines, Men, and Missions

On September 5, 1939, NAA General Order NA-62 authorized the construction of 184 bombers and one initial test airframe: B-25-NA (40-2165). *NAA/Rice*

First and Last Inglewood and Kansas City Mitchells

Inglewood First B-25

The test airframe 40-2165 would become one of NAA's longest-active B-25s, since it was used for testing until November 1942, when was modified for use as a company transport, "Whiskey Express," and would be used as a transport until January 8, 1945, when it was damaged beyond repair in a crash landing caused by a hydraulic system failure, and was scrapped. *NAA*

During preflight taxi testing, a problem with the design of the nosewheel shimmy damper resulted in a nose gear failure, damaging the aircraft. The aircraft was repaired and the shimmy damper redesigned. On August 19, 1940, test pilot Vance Breese flew 40-2165 on its maiden flight and reported that a severe roll-yaw (Dutch roll) condition existed. Later, during an early flight test, a fuel line rupture caused a small explosion, forcing a successful wheels-up landing at Mines Field. The plane was repaired again, and testing continued. *Both photos, NAA/Rice*

Last NAA Inglewood B-25, "Bones"

The bomber was allowed to arrive in India with the signatures during November 1944. While assigned to the 82nd Bomb Squadron, 12th Bomb Group, it flew several successful missions, but just before the end of the war, *Bones* was involved in a low-altitude midair collision with a large vulture and never again flew combat, and it was reported to have been scrapped in India. *AAF*

30,000th NAA Aircraft Manufactured

The B-25H-10-NA (43-5104), "Bones," was completed in July 1944, and as it neared completion, NAA employees covered the aircraft with dollar bills, which were donated to the Army-Navy relief fund. During the ceremony, employees painted their signatures on the historic aircraft. *Right, NAA; left, NAA/Rice*

The 30,000th aircraft built by NAA during the war, Mitchell B-25J-20-NC (45-8899), was ceremoniously delivered to the AAF on October 6, 1944, during the "E" Production Award ceremony. The aircraft was assigned to the 499th Bomb Squadron, 345th Bomb Group, in the Philippines and was lost on January 26, 1945, returning from a mission against Cabcaben Airfield, Bataan. The aircraft lost an engine during a landing attempt and was ditched off Tacloban, with no serious injuries to the crew. *NAA*

First Kansas City B-25

Last Kansas City B-25D

On December 22, 1941, the first Kansas City (NC) B-25D-NC bomber was completed and was quickly painted overnight before its christening and a visit from then senator Harry S. Truman the next day. Enid Bender, wife of the first factory employee, christened the aircraft as "Miss Greater Kansas City." Test pilot Paul Balfour was at the controls of "Miss Greater Kansas City" for her first flight on January 3, 1942. *NAA*

The last B-25D-35-NC, 43-3869, was completed on March 9, 1944, and like during the Inglewood "Bones" celebration, employees taped dollar bills to its fuselage, to be donated to a war bond drive. After rollout the bomber was sent to the Fairfax Modification Center for acceptance to by the Netherland East Indies Air Force. But 43-3869 was never used by the Dutch and was transferred to the Australian RAAF as A47-25 and would fly fifty-eight missions for No. 2 Squadron as KOJ. *NAA*

The delivery of "Miss Greater Kansas City" had been a tortuous one, since the Fairfax plant was not originally planned as a manufacturing plant and the first 100 Mitchells were assembled from B-25C parts in an uncompleted factory, with no assembly line or heat during what was then winter. After its rollout, the bomber was accepted on February 17, 1942, by the AAF for extended testing and was finally assigned to La Junta, Colorado, as a trainer, where it spent the remainder of the war before being scrapped during July 1945. *NAA*

Last Kansas City B-25J

NAA took souvenir photos of employees posing with their last creation, B-25J-35-NC (45-8899), which was completed on October 15, 1945, two months after NAA received official notification to cease B-25 production. On August 15, it had been determined that any aircraft that had engines already mounted would be completed, and all others would be scrapped. At that time there were seventy-two B-25J-35-NCs in final assembly, from the engine-mounting station forward, and 45-8899 was the last to have engines installed. On October 31, 1945, 45-8899 was flown along with the remaining B-25J-35-NC bombers to storage. *NAA*

On August 20, 1945, all but 2,337 Fairfax workers were laid off, with the remaining employees to begin scrapping the engineless bombers as well as completing the very last Mitchells. General Motors was eager to use the Kansas City factory to gear up for the anticipated postwar deluge of automobile orders. GM began retooling the plant for the Buick/Oldsmobile/Pontiac production division on December 1, 1945, and their first auto was ready in June 1946. The plant was later used to build F-84 Thunderstreaks during the Korean War and was abandoned in 1987 and replaced by GM with a new billion-dollar plant. *GM*

North American Test Pilots

Test pilots D. W. "Tommy" Tomlinson (*second from right*) and Paul Balfour (*left*) stand before the XB-21. Tomlinson, a contract test pilot, would first fly the NA-21 on January 1, 1937. Balfour would be the chief test pilot on the NA-40 during January 1939, and made the first flight in the B-25D on January 3, 1942. *NAA*

Vance Breese was an independent test pilot contracted by NAA to test the first B-25 in August 1940. During the 1930s and early 1940s few aircraft companies could afford a full-time test department and it was common practice for companies to hire free-lance test pilots who demanded very high fees. *NAA*

NAA Company test pilot, Ed Virgin (*left*) and test engineer, Roy Ferren, pose in the XB-24G cockpit during October 1942. Virgin would be the B-25's most prolific test pilot, logging first flights in the B-25A (2/25/1941), B-25C (11/9/1941), B-24G (10/22/1942), and XB-24H (5/15/1943). *NAA*

Royce Mission: The First B-25 Attack of the War

The Royce Mission, led by General Ralph Royce, consisted of ten B-25Cs, appropriated from the Dutch order, and three B-17s. In mid-April the mission flew from Darwin, Australia, using bomb bay fuel tanks, to staging auxiliary fields located nearby Del Monte Airfield on Mindanao. Led by Col. John Davies, B-25s from the 13th and 90th Bomb Squadrons of the 3rd Bomb Group flew a bombing strike on April 12 and two more, early morning and afternoon, on the thirteenth, which included attacks on Nichol's Field, Luzon; Cebu docks and ships in the harbor; and the Davao dock area and nearby installations. The Mitchells were involved in over twenty sorties, allegedly shooting down three enemy aircraft and sinking one Japanese transport and possibly two others. While one B-17 was destroyed and the other two severely damaged on the ground, the B-25s succeed in escaping Japanese bombing because they had been dispersed to more-concealed airfields. All the Mitchells returned to Australia without loss, evacuating important military and diplomatic personnel from Del Monte. The April 18, 1942, Doolittle Raid, five days later, eclipsed the morale-boosting accomplishments of the Royce Mission.

Lt. Col. John Davies and his crew. Note flak holes in tail fin. *AAF*

Maj. Gen. R. B. Lincoln awards the Distinguished Service Cross to the mission leader, Brig. Gen. Ralph Royce, and Lt. Col. John Davies. *AAF*

Doolittle and the Mission That Made the Mitchell Famous

James "Jimmy" Doolittle, shown here with NAA's Dutch Kindelberger, not only was a pioneering aviator, test pilot, and air racer but also was a brilliant aeronautical engineer. He received his MS degree in aeronautics from MIT in June 1924 in one year (of a scheduled two), and his 1925 aeronautical engineering doctorate was the first ever issued in the US. Doolittle's most important contribution to aeronautical technology was the development of instrument flying.

The sixteen bombers employed on the Doolittle Raid were all B-25B models, which were diverted to the Mid-Continent Airlines Modification Center, Minneapolis, Minnesota (*pictured*). Modifications were implemented for weight saving and increasing the fuel load (from 646 to 1,141 gallons). Other modifications included installation of deicers and anti-icers, removal of the liaison radio set (weight), installation of a 160-gallon collapsible neoprene auxiliary fuel tank fixed to the top of the bomb bay, and support mounts for additional fuel cells located in the bomb bay, crawlway, and lower turret area.

Beginning on March 1, 1942, the selected twenty volunteer crews and twenty-four B-25Bs from 17th Bomb Group (Medium) were to receive intensive training at Eglin Field, Florida, in simulated carrier deck takeoffs, low-level and night flying, low-altitude bombing, and overwater navigation. After extensive practice the crewmen were able to lift off as slowly as 75 mph, if aided by headwinds, with as little as 250 feet of runway before reaching the markers that indicated the end of the carrier deck. *AAF*

Lt. Ted Lawson's B-25, "Ruptured Duck" (40-2261), at Eglin. After bombing Tokyo, Lawson ditched the bomber off the China coast, losing a leg and suffering other serious injuries. But like most of the B-25 crews that came down in China, he eventually made it to safety with the help of Chinese civilians and soldiers, who suffered terrible Japanese reprisals afterward. After the Doolittle Raid, he authored *Thirty Seconds over Tokyo*, an account of his participation in the Doolittle Raid, which was later adapted into a movie of the same name. *AAF*

Because the top-secret Norden bombsight was ineffective below 4,000 feet and could be captured, the "Mark Twain," an inexpensive ($0.20), simple bar-and-plate sighting apparatus, was devised instead by Raider pilot Capt. Ross Greening.

The ventral gun turret was removed from the Doolittle Mitchells, saving 700 pounds. To enhance the inadequate Mitchell defense without adding any weight, Doolittle's celebrated "broomstick 50s" were mounted in each aircraft's clear tail cone. The ruse went so far as to paint black slots on the gun broomstick "gun barrels." The photo also shows the steel blast plates mounted on the fuselage around the dorsal turret. *AAF*

Doolittle (*left*) and *Hornet* (CV-8) commander Adm. Marc Mitscher, surrounded by the "Raiders," were photographed before the mission. After the epic raid, *Hornet* then sailed to reinforce US Navy units following the Battle of Coral Sea and was later recalled to Pearl Harbor in mid-May to take part in the Battle of Midway (June 4–6, 1942) and was sunk on October 26, 1942, during the Battle of the Santa Cruz Islands. *AAF*

Doolittle ceremonially attaches Japanese military medals to a 500-pound bomb. The B-25 bombload was a mix of three 500-pound general-purpose, high-explosive bombs and a bundle of smaller incendiaries. Two bombers also had cameras mounted to record the results of bombing. *AAF*

USS *Hornet* passed under the Golden Gate Bridge in broad daylight on April 2, 1942, with the Mitchells lashed to the carrier's flight deck in plain sight. Deck space for the B-25 was made by storing the carrier's fighters below in the hangar decks. Initial takeoffs would be limited, since much of *Hornet*'s 814-by-860-foot fight deck was taken up by the lashed bombers. *AAF*

Lt. Col. Doolittle's B-25 being positioned forward for takeoff to lead the raid on Japan. *AAF*

Iconic photo of one of Doolittle's Mitchells leaving the *Hornet*'s flight deck in windy, foul weather, which stirred up 30-foot waves that sprayed onto the flight deck. The carrier turned into high winds at 35 knots for takeoff, with its bow undulating up and down in the heavy seas. Takeoffs, actually aided by the high winds, were calculated so that the Mitchell would reach the end of the deck just when the bow was at its highest. At 0820 the first bomber took off, and an hour later, without incident, all B-25s were headed for Japan, since their hours of practice had paid high dividends. *AAF*

A B-25 passes over two large vessels at Yokosuka Naval Base. The aircraft began arriving over Japan about noon Tokyo time, six hours after launch, climbed to 1,500 feet, and bombed ten military and industrial targets in Tokyo, two in Yokohama, and one each in Yokosuka, Nagoya, Kobe, and Osaka. *AAF*

Doolittle sits on the wreckage of his Mitchell with his back to the camera somewhere in China after the raid on Tokyo. *AAF*

In June 1942, Brig. Gen. Jimmy Doolittle, promoted two ranks following the Tokyo raid, thanks NAA Inglewood workers for their support. *AAF*

Other Mitchells on Carriers

The Doolittle Raid Mitchells were not the first or the only B-25s to take off from an aircraft carrier.

February 2, 1942: USS *Hornet* (CV-8)

Ground tests had determined that a B-25 could take off using the available deck space on a then modern aircraft carrier, but actual confirmation was required. Three B-25Bs arrived a week prior to their meeting with the newly commissioned (October 20, 1941) *Hornet*'s scheduled arrival in Norfolk, Virginia, from its shakedown cruise. The crews spent the week practicing their short-field takeoff technique, but one B-25 lost an engine during practice and could not be repaired in time. During the morning of February 2, 1942, the two remaining B-25B bombers were loaded on *Hornet*'s deck and Lt. John Fitzgerald launched without incident. Twenty minutes later, Lt. James McCarthy used only 275 feet of the carrier deck to fly his B-25 into the air. Neither pilot would participate in the April Doolittle raid. *AAF*

November 15, 1944: USS *Shangri La* (CV-38)

Late In the war, aircraft were loaded aboard carriers by cranes for transport to combat areas and then similarly unloaded onto docks at their destination. But often, crane access was limited, as were suitable runways near the ports. A solution seemed to be catapulting aircraft from carriers, and many types of aircraft were tested, including PBJ-1H (BuNo 3527; former 43-4700), which was modified for carrier-landing (*left*) and catapult-launching (*right*) trials at sea. The bomber was structurally modified at the Kansas City Modification Center, with the tailhook gear modified from a Douglas SBD gear. On November 15, 1944, Lt. Cmdr. H. Sydney Bottomley headed toward USS *Shangri La* (CV-38) to make the first carrier landing by a B-25 and then taxied to the catapult position and launched and repeated the procedure for the second time before the flight back to Norfolk. As Japanese retreated back toward Tokyo, the necessity for a carrier-based variant of the B-25 was no longer necessary. *Both photos, USN*

August 29 and October 6, 1995: USS *Carl Vinson* (CVN-70)

Carrier-borne Mitchells participated in a two-part fiftieth-anniversary commemoration of the end of World War II. USS *Carl Vinson* embarked off Oahu, Hawaii, with eleven vintage World War II warbird aircraft on August 29, including the B-25Js: "Buck U" (44-30832), "In the Mood" (44-29199), and "Pacific Princess" (43-28204). During the October 6 event off the Golden Gate Bridge, seven warbirds were present on deck, including "In the Mood"; "Pacific Princess" also returned, and these two were joined by "Tootsie" (43-28204). All three B-25s took off under their own power during both events. *USN*

April 18, 1992: USS *Ranger* (CV-61)

To commemorate the Doolittle Raid's fiftieth anniversary, USS *Ranger* participated in a reenactment of the raid before 1,500 invitees, including several Raiders and VIP military veterans. Two B-25J bombers had been hoisted on board at Naval Air Station North Island, San Diego, California, and took off under their own power off Point Loma. "Heavenly Body" (*left photo*) was the first to take off, followed by "In the Mood" (*right*), after which the two Mitchells circled the carrier as they formed up with five other B-25s in three elements for a missing-man formation and headed for inland bases. *USN*

September 2000: USS *Lexington* (CV-16) and USS *Constellation* (CV-64)

The filming of the movie *Pearl Harbor* employed the carriers *Lexington* and *Constellation* for the Doolittle sequence. *USN*

Mitchells Escort Japanese Surrender Aircraft

On August 19, 1945, "Betty's Dream," of the 499th "Bats Outta Hell" Bomb Squadron, was one of the two 345th Bomb Group "Air Apaches" B-25J gunships assigned the special honor of escorting enemy Betty bombers, carrying Japanese officers and envoys from Tokyo to Ie Shima Island, off Okinawa. After a brief stay, the Japanese officials were to board AAF C-54s to be transported on to Manila to meet with Gen. Douglas MacArthur for surrender signings. *AAF*

A Mitchell and B-17 with P-38 Lightnings providing top cover, because some reluctant Japanese officials had ordered the vestiges of the Japanese army air force to shoot down their own bombers rather than surrender. The C-54s returned from Manila to Ie Shima the next day, and the Japanese officials and the signed surrender documents reboarded one Betty (the other crashed) and returned to Tokyo on August 20. *AAF*

The two Bettys were hastily painted with an all-white surrender scheme with green cross markings (instead of the Hinomaru "meat balls") on both sides of the wings, as well as on the vertical stabilizer and rear fuselage. One Betty was a former G6M1 transport, while the other was a disarmed G4M1 bomber. MacArthur deliberately and mockingly allocated the Bettys the call signs "Bataan 1" and "Bataan 2." *Aviation History Online Museum*

B-25s from the 501st Bomb Squadron of the Air Apaches escorted Mitsubishi Betty surrender aircraft en route to Ie Shima, in August 1945. *AAF*

Mother Nature Destroys Seventy-Four Mitchells

The AAF's largest single-day loss to date occurred on March 22–23, 1944, when seventy-four 340th Bomb Group Mitchells were destroyed on the ground at Pompeii Air Field, Italy; fourteen more were less damaged and eventually repaired. Improbably, the success could not be credited to the Luftwaffe but to Mount Vesuvius, which erupted, dropping rocks and hot volcanic debris on the base, 5 miles away. Previously, sixty-four aircraft had been lost at Pearl Harbor; sixty on the August 17, 1943, Regensburg-Schweinfurt mission; and fifty-four in bombing Ploesti on August 1, 1943. *AAF*

Nazi propaganda broadcaster Axis Sally reported that the 340th was knocked out of the war, in a clear sign that God had sided with the Germans! However, when the 340th moved to Paestum, 40 miles away, God reequipped the unit, which was back in action five days later. The later Operation Bodenplatte, a Luftwaffe surprise attack on January 1, 1945, far surpassed the Vesuvius total, with 290 destroyed and 180 damaged on the ground. *AAF*

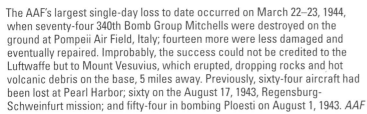

Although dispersed to prevent extensive damage from Luftwaffe air attack this B-25 and all Mitchells of the 340th Bomb Group was parked in a blanket of ash over its wheels and suffered smashed Plexiglas, burned fabric off all control surfaces, and melted tires. Despite all its aircraft being destroyed the 340th borrowed aircraft and flew its next scheduled mission. *AAF*

B-25 Collides with the Empire State Building

On July 28, 1945, Lt. Col. William Smith was flying a B-25D-15-NC (41-30577) on a flight from Bedford, Massachusetts, to Newark, New Jersey. "Old John Feather Merchant" had been used as a trainer for the 12th Air Force in North Africa, and during June 1945 it was converted to a VIP Military Air Transport Command transport. Just prior to leaving Bedford, Lt. Col. Smith was informed that due to the weather he would have to fly by instruments or visually. During the turbulent flight, he descended to 800 feet while over Queens to remain in sight of the ground. Smith thought he was on course to land at Newark but found himself actually flying through the streets of New York City. The Mitchell flew down 42nd Street and then turned south at about 5th Street, placing the bomber on a collision course with the Empire State Building. *AAF*

At approximately 0950, the B-25 pulled up and banked hard but crashed between the Empire State Building's seventy-eighth and seventy-ninth floors. The Mitchell ripped into pieces, cascading burning fuel down the side of the building; one engine crashed through the building and landed on the street below. The three crewmen of the B-25 were killed along with eleven office workers, and twenty-six were injured. Despite major damage to the seventy-eighth, seventy-ninth, and eightieth floors, the building's main structure was not severely damaged. *AAF*

B-25 Medal of Honor Recipients

Lt. Col. James Doolittle

On May 19, 1942, at the time as a brigadier general, Doolittle was awarded the Medal of Honor: "For conspicuous leadership above the call of duty, involving personal valor and intrepidity at an extreme hazard to life. With apparent certainty of being forced to land in enemy territory or perish at sea, Gen. Doolittle personally led a squadron of bombers, manned by volunteer crews, in a highly destructive on the Japanese mainland."

After the raid on Tokyo, Doolittle crash-landed his B-25 in friendly territory north of Quzhou, China. He is pictured here (third from right front row) with members of his flight crew and local Chinese officials. Richard "Dick" Cole (second from right), the last of the Doolittle Raiders, died at the age of 103 on April 9, 2019. *AAF*

Pictured are, *left to right*, President Franklin Roosevelt; Lt. Gen. Hap Arnold; Doolittle's wife, Josephine; Doolittle; and the chief of staff, Gen. George Marshall. All of the other Raiders received the Distinguished Flying Cross. In addition, Lt. (Dr.) Thomas White, who amputated pilot Lt. Ted Lawson's leg, and Cpl. David Thatcher, engineer-gunner on Lawson's crew, were awarded the Silver Star for their aid to the wounded. On May 19, 2014, the US House of Representatives voted to award all Doolittle Raiders a Congressional Gold Medal, for "outstanding heroism, valor, skill, and service to the United States in conducting the bombings of Tokyo." The award ceremony took place at the Capitol Building on April 15, 2015. During the war, Doolittle would be promoted to lieutenant general and commanded the 12th Air Force over North Africa, the 15th Air Force over the Mediterranean, and the 8th Air Force over Europe. He was awarded the four-star general rank in 1985 and passed away at age ninety-six in 1993. *AAF*

Maj. Ralph Cheli
(405th Bomb Squadron, 38th Bomb Group)

On August 18, 1943, Maj. Ralph Cheli, the commanding officer of the 405th Bomb Squadron, 38th Bomb Group, led a group of Mitchells on a low-level attack on two Japanese airfields near Wewak, New Guinea. Although Cheli's bomber was severely damaged by enemy interceptors, he elected not to bail out of his burning bomber and led his unit in an organized, successful attack. After crash-landing in the sea, he was taken a prisoner of war and was later either executed on Rabaul or lost at sea while being transported to Japan. During this time when his status was unknown, Cheli was awarded the Medal of Honor, posthumously, on October 28, 1943. *AAF*

Maj. Raymond Wilkins
(8th Bomb Squadron, 3rd Bomb Group)

On November 2, 1943, Maj. Raymond Wilkins, the CO of the 8th Bomb Squadron, 3rd Bomb Group, 3rd Attack Group, led his B-25 squadron on a bombing raid on enemy shipping near Rabaul, New Britain. Wilkins's bomber was immediately hit by antiaircraft fire, but he decided not turn around but, as the lead bomber, continued to direct the attack to the target. While repeatedly exposed to intense AA fire, he successfully strafed and bombed, destroying two enemy vessels. Despite severe damage to his aircraft, he had continued to attack until his Mitchell was shot down and crashed into the sea, killing the crew. Wilkins was posthumously awarded the Medal of Honor on March 24, 1944. *AAF*

Mitchell Women

Due to the Great Depression, women had little presence in the prewar labor force, but as the military draft removed more men from the factories, women became the major labor source. In order to recruit women for factory jobs, a propaganda campaign was created that centered on the tough yet feminine "Rosie the Riveter."

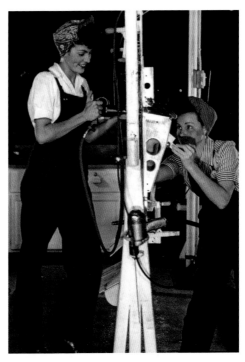

Frances Perkins, an American sociologist and workers'-rights advocate, was the longest-serving secretary of labor (1933 to 1945) and the first woman appointed to the US Cabinet. In this position she was instrumental in bringing women into the American labor market. She is pictured visiting the NAA Kansas City factory. *NAA*

The iconic Rosie the Riveter stereotypes, head bandannas and all, are carefully posed to demonstrate that a women could do a man's job. The photo on the right is posed, with the man in the photo participating as the bucker, which was considered the lesser riveting job. *Both photos, LoC*

Keeping American women looking their best was thought to be important both for men's and women's morale. To alleviate concerns that the demands of factory work would make women too masculine, cosmetics were never rationed during the war, and some factories even provided female employees with lessons in how to apply makeup. Initially, a one-piece denim overall was selected as appropriate factory wear, but as time passed, overalls or slacks with a suitable work blouse became standard. *All photos, LoC*

However, there were photos that depicted women doing "women's work," such as heat-sealing (i.e., ironing) the seams of a self-sealing fuel tank. *LoC*

B-25s in the Movies

Thirty Seconds over Tokyo

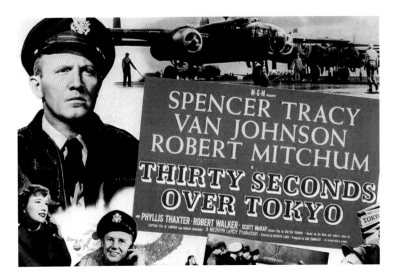

Thirty Seconds over Tokyo: Of all the studio movies released during World War II, MGM's *Thirty Seconds over Tokyo* is one of the most credible, having documentary quality. It was the story of the April 1942 Doolittle Tokyo raid, faithfully based and adapted from Capt. Ted Lawson's bestselling book of the same name. The story line followed Lawson and his crew in their B-25, the "Ruptured Duck," in a "powerful account of the preparation, implementation, and aftermath of the mission." The film, released in November 1944, was produced by Sam Zimbalist and directed by Mervyn LeRoy. Spencer Tracy played the role of Jimmy Doolittle; Van Johnson was pilot Lt. Ted Lawson. *Author/MGM*

LeRoy gathered crews and twelve B-25Cs and Ds from the 336th and 952nd Twin-Engine Flight Training Squadrons, based at Mather Field, California. Aerial production began in mid-February 1944, filming the most-important and most-dramatic scenes of the short-field takeoff sequences at Hurlburt/Eglin Fields, Florida. An actual carrier was unavailable, so carrier scenes were shot on a 135-foot replica of USS *Hornet*'s flight deck built on the largest MGM soundstage (*shown*). Three of the B-25s from the Hurlburt/Eglin shoot were towed on the set, their engines were started, and they were crewed by actors. *Author/MGM*

The filmed takeoffs were a skillful mix of newsreel footage and radio-controlled, 1-inch-to-1-foot Mitchell miniatures created by the MGM special-effects department. The miniature B-25s and *Hornet* were placed in a 300-square-foot water tank that was equipped with pumps and wave machines. The B-25 miniatures were filmed as they were launched off the carrier flight deck along a piano wire, which was projected on the studio screen with the actors standing in front of it. *Author/MGM*

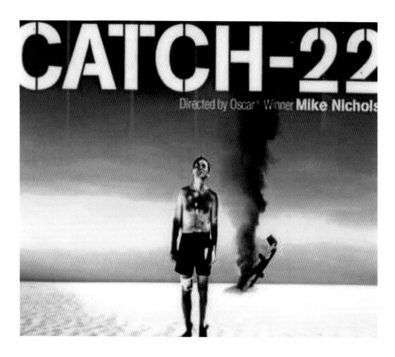

In 1970, Paramount Pictures' director Mike Nichols filmed an ambitious adaptation of Joseph Heller's bestselling masterpiece of the mid-1950s, the very black comedy *Catch-22*, set against the background of 12th Air Force B-25 operations from World War II Italy. Heller had been a wartime B-25 bombardier with the 488th Bomb Squadron, 340th Bomb Group, and his antiwar novel was a popular choice for a movie, considering the antiwar, antimilitary sentiment rampant in the US at the time. *Author/Paramount*

The mixed batch of B-25s that Tallman acquired had had their turrets and turret rings previously removed, and he needed to locate and purchase a number of surplus turrets. Tallman was scrupulous about the correct placement of the Js' and Ds' turrets, on either the top of the forward or rear fuselage, respectively. Aided by the Paramount special-effects department, dummy machine guns were installed and a method of revolving the turrets was devised, using an automobile steering wheel. Pictured are a studio B-25 mockup and how the scene appeared in the movie. *Author/Paramount*

Pilot/star Harrison Ford poses before taking off in a movie mission. Although AAF B-25s were prominently featured in *Hanover Street*, in actuality the bomber was not used over northern Europe during the war; the medium-bomber role there was assumed by the B-26. The filmmakers were forced to use the B-25 since there were few B-26 Marauders in existence. *Author/Columbia*

Hanover Street is a 1979 Columbia Pictures World War II adventure-romance directed by Peter Hyams and starring Harrison Ford as an American bomber pilot stationed in London who becomes romantically involved with a married British nurse (Lesley-Anne Down). He then improbably finds himself on a spy mission with the nurse's husband (Christopher Plummer). *Author/Columbia*

All five B-25Js in *Hanover Street* were staged in formation for the opening raid sequence, the first time since 1970's *Catch-22* that a massed aerial sequence of B-25s was filmed. The aerial sequences were filmed mostly at the by-then-disused UK Bovingdon Airfield, using five Mitchells specially flown to England from America for the filming. After the filming, four of the five Mitchells were sent to air museums in Brussels, Madrid, RAF Hendon, and Grissom in California. The other perished in a hangar fire. *Author/Columbia*

A Guy Named Joe is a 1943 MGM film release starring Spencer Tracy, a "reckless" B-25 pilot flying out of England. He is in love with WASP pilot Irene Dunne, who begs him to accept a transfer back to the US, but he flies one last mission to recon a German aircraft carrier! He is wounded and bails out into the sea to then find himself walking in the clouds, where he meets with "the General," who sends him back to Earth. After a series of complicated plot turns, he unites Dunne with new pilot Van Johnson. When Dunne finds that Johnson was to fly an extremely dangerous mission to destroy the "largest Japanese ammunition dump in the Pacific," she steals his aircraft. Tracy guides her in completing the mission and returning to the base to Johnson, and Tracy walks away, "his job done." *MGM*

Tracy is depicted in a courageous publicity pose in a B-25 mockup cockpit. *MGM*

B-25s were mostly shown flying background shots, but the film's highlight was a special-effects scale model B-25 (*pictured*), supposedly showing Tracy crashing his B-25 into a completely fictitious German aircraft carrier. The film was set in the ETO and used Mitchells even though none were stationed there. *MGM*

As a morale booster, Hollywood dispatched its biggest stars to visit the front lines. It was much more arduous to visit the primitive South Pacific bases compared to comfortable bases in the UK. Pictured is actor Gary Cooper with pilots of 90th Bomb Squadron, 3rd Bomb Group, and B-25D "Here's Howe" at Dobodura Airfield, Australian Papua, in mid-1943. *AAF*

SSgt. Charlton Heston enlisted in the AAF in 1944 and served for two years as a radio operator and aerial gunner aboard a B-25 Mitchell stationed in the Alaskan Aleutian Islands with the 77th Bomb Squadron, 11th Air Force. *Author*

Three's Company's Mr. Roper, Norman Fell, served as a B-25 tail gunner in the Pacific. *Author*

Tallmantz Aviation

Over the years, Hollywood engaged many Mitchells, either in front of or behind the camera. In organizing Tallmantz Aviation Company in 1961, renowned aerial cinematographer Frank Tallman employed ex-B-25J (44-30823/N1042B) and ex-B-25H (43-4643/N1203) as camera aircraft. The camera plane was operated by a three-person flight crew, while four camera operators worked cameras in various locations, including the large transparent nose area installed for Cinerama filming. *Author*

Tallman used Mitchell camera ships for such movies as *Flight of the Phoenix*, *Memphis Belle*, *How the West Was Won*, *It's a Mad Mad Mad World*, *Battle of Britain*, and *633 Squadron*. Depicted is the camera ship painted in camouflage so as to blend into the formation while filming *Catch-22* sequences. *Author*

"Photo Fanny"

Built as B-25J-25 (44-30423), the Planes of Fame's B-25 "Photo Fanny" was first seen in front of the camera during 1977 in the television series *Baa Baa Black Sheep*, and in such films as *Always*, *Forever Young*, *1941*, and *Pearl Harbor*. The plane's television credits included *Simon and Simon*, *Highway to Heaven*, and several commercials. For her role as a camera ship, "Fanny" was modified with a bubble dome installed in the top turret location, camera mounts, portable video screens, and the camera nose, which can be mounted to replace the original greenhouse nose as required. Fanny's camera ship credits include *Con Air*, *Air Force One*, *Drop Zone*, *Executive Decision*, and *Forever Young*. *Planes of Fame*

The Only Mitchell to Fly Combat Out of in England in WWII

Black American B-25 Unit

Despite Hollywood B-25 film characterizations in *A Guy Named Joe* and *Hanover Street*, the only AAF Mitchell to fly in the ETO from England was a B-25C-5 (42-53357) that was originally assigned to the 310th Bomb Group, probably to form the nucleus of a projected B-25 combat group in the 8th Air Force's 3rd Bomb Wing. When the 8th and 9th Air Forces chose the B-26 to operate as the medium bomber in the ETO, 42-53357 was sent to 8th Air Force HQ as a communications aircraft, where it was dubbed "Miss Nashville." During September 1943, it was transferred to the 7th Photo Group, where it was used as a hack, and for dual instruction training of F-5 Lightning photo-recon pilots. Lt. Gen. James Doolittle, 8th Air Force CG, flew this Mitchell for a short time, probably bringing back memories of his raid on Tokyo. The bomber was sent to the 25th Bomb Group, which painted it black and added invasion stripes. From June 5, 1944, it flew thirteen night photo missions to detect V-1 launching sites. After this combat stint, it served as a courier aircraft, transporting photographs to bases in the UK and France. On October 26, 1944, it was mistakenly fired on by friendly AA guns near Chalon-sur-Seine airfield and caught fire and skidded off the runway, killing the pilot and flight engineer and badly injuring the copilot. *AAF*

On May 13, 1943, an all-Black medium bomber unit was constituted in the 477th Bomb Group and assigned to the 3rd Air Force. Although its initial training was on Martin B-26s, the unit was soon redesignated as the 477th Composite Group, 1st Air Force, flying one P-47 and four B-25 squadrons. However, training was only underway when the war ended. *AAF*

NAA in the Postwar

Mitchell Final Disposition

This B-25H (43-4897) was one of approximately sixty-four Mitchells awaiting disposal at Kingman, Arizona. *William Larkins*

Hundreds of PBJs await scrapping at the NAS Clinton, Oklahoma, disposal site. On January 24, 1946, the War Assets Administration offered 1,084 Mitchells for sale. A B-25 could be purchased for $8,250, while its rival, the B-26, could be picked up for a mere $3,000. *AAF*

A B-25C (41-13266) awaits its fate at the Ontario Auxiliary Airfield, California. *William Larkins*

B-25s awaiting fate at Kingman, Arizona, scrapping facility where they were segregated by type. There are B-24s stored on right middle of photo and B-17s from the top and into the far distance. *Larkins*

Kindelberger and Atwood Lead NAA into the Postwar

James "Dutch Kindelberger

Under Dutch's guidance, NAA produced prop- and jet-powered fighters and bombers, as well as military trainers, and then developed new technologies to produce rocket engines and record-breaking rocket-powered aircraft. Between 1935 and 1967, NAA, under Kindelberger's reign, manufactured more military aircraft than any other aircraft company in US history and established its position as the prime contractor for the nation's space program. Kindelberger became NAA chairman and CEO in 1948, with Atwood replacing him as president. Kindelberger remained chairman of the board until his death at sixty-seven on July 27, 1962. Upon his death, Atwood became chairman of the board. *NAA*

Lee Atwood

Atwood (*left, with Dutch*) worked as NAA's chief engineer/executive for over thirty-five years, developing the P-51 fighter during World War II, the F-100 jet fighter, and the X-15 rocket plane and overseeing the Apollo space program. In 1960, he became NAA president and CEO when Kindelberger retired, and in 1962 he became chairman of the board following Kindelberger's death. In 1967, Atwood joined with Willard Rockwell to form North American Rockwell, being named its new president and CEO. Atwood retired in 1970 and remained on the board until 1978. He passed away on March 5, 1999. *NAA*

The B-45 Tornado was NAA's and America's first production postwar jet bomber and the new USAF's first operational jet bomber. As the first jet bomber capable of carrying an atomic bomb and the first multijet aircraft to refuel in midair, it played an important initial role as America's Cold War nuclear deterrent for several years in the early 1950s.

In America's response to the new German jet bombers, the development of the B-45 began as NAA's NA-130 proposal on September 8, 1944. NAA built three prototypes that would be deemed superior to the rival Convair XB-46, and on January 2, 1947, a contract for immediate production of B-45As was authorized. However, the B-45's future became uncertain once the Boeing B-47 Stratojet's development accelerated and its flight testing showed positive results. During mid-1948, budget restraints reduced Air Force expenditure. The B-45 production run of 190 was reduced, and ninety-four B-45As, ten B-45C bomber versions, and thirty-three RB-45 reconnaissance versions were built. *NAA*

Although chronically beset by engine problems along with numerous other minor flaws, the B-45 would recoup importance when America entered the Korean War in 1950, during which it proved its worth both as a bomber and as a reconnaissance aircraft. Postwar it continued its recon role, and a 91st Reconnaissance Wing RB-45 flew from Alaska to Japan in nine hours, fifty minutes to win the MacKay Trophy. By the end of the 1950s, all B-45s had been removed from active service, and both it and, later, the B-47 were replaced by the supersonic Convair B-58 Hustler. *NAA*

The B-45 was North American's bomber swan song, but the company's Korean War MiG killer, the F-86 Sabre, is considered as one of the greatest fighter aircraft of all time. It entered service with the USAF in 1949, and during its production run, about 6,200 Sabres were built in the US and 3,660 more were built by twenty-five other countries before production ceased in December 1956.